"Each instrumental teacher is in fact their own small music business. Learning how to run their business effectively is a vital endeavour, and an often overlooked one. In *Music Teaching Made Profitable*, music business owners learn about the different stages of music studio growth, various elements to consider at each stage and how to achieve growth. Wendy generously shares her experiences as an instrumental teacher, music studio owner and business coach for anyone who seeks a clearer path through the Music Studio Business world!"

Carly McDonald
Creative Editor – The Piano Teacher
Owner Nova Music

"I would highly recommend Wendy to anyone who wants help with growing their music business. Wendy has been working in the music teaching business for years (over 30 I think) and is a wealth of knowledge on everything to do with running a music teaching business. She is never one to sit still and is always looking at ways to extend and improve. She is highly efficient, a great communicator, extremely reliable and has a great personality. She has now become my mentor and I feel very lucky to have her there to guide me along my musical journey".

Cath Dowling
Owner Kids on Key

PRAISE FOR THE AUTHOR

"Teaching music is a labour of love, and this book has a wealth of information on setting up the ideal conditions for music teaching studios to thrive. Wendy Brentnall-Wood shares her in-depth knowledge and writes with experience and enthusiasm. A great read and essential reference for all Music Teachers."

Helen Tuckey
Australian Strings Association National President

"One of the biggest challenges facing Music Teachers around the world is knowing how to run the business side of their studio. Teacher training courses seldom teach these skills, leaving musicians woefully unprepared for success in a competitive industry. Even more distressing is hearing older teachers actively discouraging graduates from setting up studios because of their own struggles to make ends meet. Well, all this is about to change with the release of Wendy's new book: *Music Teaching Made Profitable*, a resource that will change people's perceptions of how they can generate a more reliable, steady income from music teaching and how to grow a more profitable business to support them in the future."

Tim Topham
Director, Top Music Education PTY LTD

"Wendy came to talk to teachers at our pedagogy conference about how they could build their teaching practices into successful businesses. Her presentation was so well received that we invited her back to advise our teachers on strategies for creating their own teaching programmes. Her ideas were inspirational and easily tailored to each teacher's unique goals and aspirations.

Wendy's new book is a comprehensive and practical guide to business success, gleaned from her own multifaceted experience as a musician, teacher, author, publisher and business owner. I encourage all Music Teachers to read it!"

Jocelyn (Jo) Kotchie
Composer, Music Educator and President of the West Australian Music Teachers' Association

"Instrumental Music Teachers start out with a love of music and performance skills, and wanting to share their knowledge and skills with others beginning a career in teaching. Most however have little or no knowledge of the business skills necessary to facilitate this career path. Wendy Brentnall-Wood's book fills a much needed niche; I would recommend it for all teachers to expand their business knowledge both starting out and growing a music teaching practice."

Margaret Schlink
Violin and Viola Teacher, Director of Perth Scottish Fiddlers
AMusA (viola), DipMusT, MMusPS | Accred WAMTA Member |
Past President AUSTA WA

Mu$ic Teaching Made Profitable

Global Publishing Group
Australia • New Zealand • Singapore • America • London

Mu$ic Teaching Made Profitable

An Expert's Guide to Generating More Income as a Music Teacher

Wendy Brentnall-Wood

First Edition 2019

Illustrations by Cara Brentnall

National Library of Australia
Cataloguing-in-Publication entry:

Music Teaching Made Profitable: An Expert's Guide to Generating More Income as a Music Teacher - Wendy Brentnall-Wood

1st ed.
ISBN: 978-1-925288-84-1 (pbk.)

A catalogue record for this book is available from the National Library of Australia

Published by Global Publishing Group
PO Box 517 Mt Evelyn, Victoria 3796 Australia
Email Info@GlobalPublishingGroup.com.au

For further information about orders:
Phone: +61 3 9739 4686 or Fax +61 3 8648 6871

This Book is dedicated to Howard Brentnall, my incredibly supportive husband of over 30 years.

Howard has helped support my career and business through "hands on" work of all sorts. Assisting at concerts, managing our retail and financial divisions, managing and maintaining retail premises and so many other essential tasks, all this when employed full time elsewhere.

His readiness to help me achieve my goals and dreams has also been demonstrated by his willingness to do whatever it takes to keep family and household running smoothly and allow me to spend my time developing my dreams.

Perhaps more importantly Howard has earned an extra accolade here as even after 34 years, he still manages to listen with great patience to my creative rambling conversations as new ideas and projects get me excited and my creative juices firing!

Deepest Thanks!

I hope we can have many more years and adventures together!

Wendy Brentnall-Wood

ACKNOWLEDGEMENTS

This book is the result of the influence and support of many, many people over my entire life.

I am absolutely sure that I would not have had the confidence or ability to achieve what I have done throughout my career, without the example set and wisdom of my father **Robert (Bob) Wood**. I have aspired to his no-nonsense, down to earth country approach to decisions, relationships and getting things done. A self-employed builder, once farmer, his entrepreneurial spirit has obviously influenced not only myself but my three entrepreneurial siblings.

Always at his side, my generous and loving mum, **Betty** was a constant encouragement to me musically and emotionally – always ready with a hug and a cup of tea! Her own achievements as a mother of four, bookkeeper, local sports champion in two sports and a musician were as inspiring to me as my dad. They were a great team.

My amazing husband **Howard Brentnall**, for always being by my side and "having my back". To my amazing, resilient, compassionate and sensitive children, **Jess**, **James** and **Cara**, I have to acknowledge your acceptance of having a mother whose career at times meant having the house turned upside down to accommodate music lessons and whose working hours were often unpredictable. I would also like to thank **Tony**, our most recent family addition for his loving care of our daughter Jess (his wife) and his interest in the development of my business.

To my long-time friends from school, university and early teaching days, I wish to thank **Jenny Bennett**, **Janette Vardy**, **Janet Stebbins** and **Cathy Georgiev** for accepting me "warts and all". Knowing that I have friends who will always be honest and whom I can call as needed is such a blessing. They have a continuing connection no matter the length of the time that passes. Their ongoing interest in my family, health and my dreams is treasured by me.

I would not have achieved the musical skills from which I have built my career had I not had the influence of my Aunt **Wilma Jennings** and long term piano teacher **May Clifford**. The experiences good and bad, that I had through a host of numerous other music teachers also have made me the teacher I am, and for those I am grateful.

I have been privileged over my decades of being in business, to connect with a number of different mentors, consultants and advisors who in their different ways have had a positive impact on me. The importance of always learning from **Roger Hamilton**, and the value of having purpose, focus and "giving back" from **Paul Dunn of B1G1** will stay with me forever.

To **Henry Perlen**, **Nicholas James**, **Tony Mirabelli**, **Angela Wong** and **Carmelo Montalto, Kip McGrath** and **Storm McGrath**, I thank you for your trusted advice over the years.

I need to also acknowledge that without the skilled tuition of **Kaye Dyson** and **Allison Brown** and the influence of **Kerwin Rae**, this last decade could have looked quite different! Their encouragement and tuition in Meditation and Pilates have enabled me to improve and maintain a level of physical and mental health that has supported my extremely busy life!

I would like to say thank you to all the staff and teachers I have employed who have helped me develop and grow my knowledge and skills. In particular I would like to acknowledge **Paul Allen**, **John Francis**, **Lucie Holden** and **Jo Callegari** who were more than employees or franchisees, they became trusted close friends whose support through some tough times went "over and above".

Last but not least a big THANK YOU to the team at Global Publishing for inspiring me and showing me that this book was possible.

BONUS OFFER

I can't possibly give you everything you need to know about becoming a successful Music Teacher in one book.

To help you continue your understanding and keep up the momentum, I've got lots of 'extra' information, tools, resources and videos available for you on my Website.

Continuing to research, to hear and see the challenges and success that other Music teachers have had, is invaluable to helping you FAST TRACK your own success.

A great starting point is this free educational webinar titled...

"Build your Dream Music School & Dream Life
- Learn the 6 Easy Steps"

Go check out all my FREE webinars here:
www.WendysMusic.com.au/webinars-wendy/

EXTRA BONUS EBOOK!!

Are you wondering how some super busy Music teachers manage to teach all day, every day, stay sane AND keep on top of all the administration, bookwork, marketing, finances and other things needed to keep their studio running?

The tricks are in the planning, organisation and keeping consistent systems!

If you would like to learn the 8 Habits of a Successful Music Teacher, then grab a copy of my eBook:

8 HABITS OF A SUCCESSFUL MUSIC TEACHER

Follow the suggestions to build yourself systems and habits that simplify your life and eliminate most of the stress.

Get your copy of the 42 page eBook here:
www.WendysMusic.com.au/8habitsebook

NB Books are usually around for a long time so if for any reason the technology isn't working for you feel free to email us for help at wmmarketing@wendysmusic.com.au.

CONTENTS

FOREWORD

Scientific research has now clearly shown the benefits of learning music at any age, but particularly from a young age. Music makes a significant impact on the neural networks like no other activity does. The impact of learning music can be higher cognitive capacity in language, problem solving, numeracy, improved concentration, improved fine motor skills and more.

Research on the mental, physical and emotional benefits of music making has advanced to a point where the innate benefits of music making are more universally known and understood.

Teaching is a fundamental thing in our society – the most honourable of callings. This book is about how to be a more successful Music Teacher. A progressive society needs to revere teaching, and in turn a teacher needs to create a place where learning can take place in a creative environment, and one not saddled with stress or disorganisation. This is where this book comes to the fore.

There are many professional musicians who teach to supplement performance income and add to the fabric of our arts society. There are many skilled and experienced musicians ready to pass on their knowledge.

To have a person of 40-years' experience offer themselves as a mentor in this field is a rare commodity in the music products industry. Anyone who has run a business knows that knowing some of the pitfalls in advance would have helped them avoid problems and made life and business easier.

This book provides practical guidance in the numerous tasks involved in setting up a teaching business from the most basic to the advanced.

Customer service skills and business acumen are essential to be a successful teacher as they are in any business.

Wendy is indeed a passionate and high achieving operator in the business of music, always proactive in retail, teaching and in business. She is well qualified to give an insight into the structures needed to effectively support a career in music education, whether that be as an individual teacher seeking to diversify their income or to someone wishing to expand an established studio.

To generate a more reliable, steady income from music teaching and how to grow a more profitable business to support a musician into the future is a common theme throughout this book.

Music and the arts are vital to every child's education. There are gaps in the provision of music education in schools, which makes private Music Teachers a vital community resource. The advice in these pages is invaluable in improving the knowledge base of Music Teachers and our industry benefits with more skilled teachers creating more music makers as we bring music into more people's lives.

Robert Walker
Executive director
Australian Music Association Inc.

PART 1

WHAT TO EXPECT FROM THIS BOOK

CHAPTER 1

INTRODUCTION

Why teach music?

This is a book for people who want to teach music but also want to do so in a profitable way to ensure they live the life of their dreams.

You might already be teaching music, or you might be at the point in your life where you've decided you would like to teach music.

You might be a musician like Paul who had been suffering in a non-music career, working in the bank since he left school, playing gigs whenever he can on weekends and basically living from weekend to weekend.

You might be a college student like Nicole, spending hours a day playing and perfecting your performing skills, hours of in-depth musical study and starting to teach a few students at a local music school to see if it's what she wants to do as a full-time career.

You could be like Peter, a musician with regular weekend gigs and week night rehearsals struggling to make enough to survive and wanting to make use of spare time, and earn extra, perhaps more reliable, income.

Perhaps you are even like Christine, a parent needing to return part time to the workforce to help the family finances, but not wanting to

compromise her own children's lifestyle and thinking that teaching from home would be the solution.

From these examples you've probably already realised that I am not referring to teaching classroom music at a school or other institution. Although I was trained as a classroom and instrumental music teacher, classroom teachers in general tend to be "salaried employees" rather than principally business owners, which is the group of people I want to help.

Perhaps you believe you have a skill that others want and would like to earn either some "extra cash" from it, or turn it into a full-time career.

Perhaps there is an element of wanting to "earn something back" from your musical skills and passion.

Perhaps it's music you love and the teaching thing is a way of being surrounded by music whilst earning money?

No matter which of these resembles your situation, I would say it's most likely that you are passionate about making music and having it in your own life.

Why do I teach music?

I am one of those people for whom a career in music was the only career I ever wanted. The choices I had at University were Music Performance, Music Teaching or I could have been one of the first years' enrolments for Music Therapy. This was the late 1970s so the choices were much fewer at that time. I was never interested in becoming a performer, in

fact I didn't and still don't enjoy performing in public as I am a very nervous performer and suffer high levels of anxiety whenever I have had to perform (something I didn't recognise until decades later). Therapy was so new and involved a lot of statistics back then, so although the idea of helping others using music had great appeal, the course itself did not, so I opted for teaching.

For me music has always been a part of daily life, something I use naturally in different ways to help me manage things like anxiety and depression, but also to energise me when exercising, relax me for sleep and to help focus and concentrate when working.

My Mum used to tell me a story of how when I was around the age of two, I would often stand under the kitchen table and sing. Apparently I thought that by standing under the table, no-one would know it was me! When I was at school I joined every singing and instrumental group that was available. I rarely had a lunchtime free due to the rehearsals, and then of course there was sometimes other rehearsals before and after school too.

In primary school we were lucky enough to have a teacher who taught us to play recorder, and I was learning piano from my aunt from age of eight also. My maternal grandparents also encouraged my love of music making by giving me a glockenspiel when I was very young — although it has slightly wonky legs, I still have that glock!

In secondary school I was able to learn clarinet and percussion and later oboe, whilst continuing formal piano and teaching myself folk guitar.

After graduating I also learnt violin in order to have some idea of how I could help students in the string orchestra I was asked to start and grow.

Then came flute, a little saxophone, trumpet and drum kit… so I guess you get the general idea that I enjoy making music!

So I started teaching music in classroom and private instrumental lessons mostly because I loved making music and listening to music myself and wanted others to have that enjoyment also.

As my career continued though, I was frustrated because I found that there are only a relatively small percentage of people who are able to maintain the discipline of learning to play an instrument. My first impressions were that this happened because the method of teaching was dry and boring — traditional teaching based on the exam syllabus and little else. In addition the way beginners were being taught back then when I started out, and often still, makes it too hard for many of them to understand, let alone ENJOY the process.

Eventually after researching and using a variety of other people's teaching methods, I wrote my own to simplify the process of teaching beginners to read and play music in an easy step by step process. I also formulated a teaching program that has now been used in my own music schools for more than a decade and which encompasses a variety of musical activities such as improvisation and performance from the very first term of learning.

My schools and programs show how to make it easy for students from age three, and students with special needs, through all ages, to learn to read and play music. It works on a variety of instruments easily and being easy makes it more enjoyable, as we all need to feel a sense of achievement in whatever activity we are undertaking.

Recently though I began wondering.

Is that it? Are these the only reasons we teach music?

There are of course people like me who always wanted to teach, not wanting to be a professional performer, but enjoy instead the satisfaction of helping others achieve and learn.

It's not uncommon to hear.

We are fortunate now that there is considerable scientific research being done to show conclusively the benefits that music has for anyone. Music uses so many different areas of the brain that it has been proven to be beneficial to children's cognitive development and therefore provides many benefits for other areas of development.

Music also can be seen as the cornerstone of social development and community.

Humans need social contact, and music provides multiple ways to strengthen social skills and contacts, whether that is singing along at a concert, dancing at a club, singing your favourite team's theme song, or celebrating a special family occasion. Everyone can join in, whether tapping the beat, singing or even playing an instrument in some sort of ensemble. The joy of making music together is almost unsurpassable.

Why focus here on "business"?

Over my rather lengthy 40 year teaching career and entrepreneurial journey (yes I am getting old!), I have been asked over and over again, and in a variety of ways how I managed to build such a successful music business. In the last few years I have been specifically sought out by colleagues for advice in different areas of school programs, retail music schools and home studios. It's been apparent to me for a long time that although we train and learn for years (if not decades) to become proficient and professional musicians, we rarely train in business management of

any sort. The trend has been, with the growth of the internet, to stumble from one website to another, read blogs, listen to webinars and podcasts in what is essentially a random way in the hope we will learn the "secret formulas" of running a business that just happens to be a music school.

If you remember the last time you learnt a new skill successfully, you will probably also remember that there was a consistent method, system or program that you followed to achieve that success. Learning to run a business needs the same consistent, systematic approach. Developing this has been what enabled me to repeatedly reinvent and grow my music education Company.

The two pillars of profitable music teaching

As I see it, to become a successful, in demand music teacher requires two key components.

1. Be a good or even great teacher and
2. Treat your teaching like a business not a hobby!

To be a great teacher requires not just knowing your subject, which in this case would be the skill of playing your instrument, and musical knowledge. It also requires the skill of communication. Adapting to different students ways of learning and communicating the universal language of music to them in a way that they can understand, enjoy and make their own.

There are lots of great teachers who struggle to make enough money from teaching because they never get around to developing their "business" skills. Maybe it's because some people see business as "cut-throat" or all about money and scared they may lose connection with their art and their students. Maybe they just don't like doing administration or finances or broadcasting themselves. I can understand that!

We all have different strengths and weaknesses and it's OK to acknowledge them. However it's not OK to just ignore things like budgets, and marketing if it means you end up living on the poverty line!

What's the Point?

One of the reasons I am now writing this book is because less than a year ago I had a small but freaky collision with cancer. I won't bore you with the details, but essentially a tiny red dot on my nose that I didn't know I had suddenly required plastic surgery to eradicate the cancer.

Why am I telling you this?

Well, essentially it was one of those episodes where a few weeks later I started to realise the extent of what had just happened – an encounter with "the Big C" — and that got me thinking about where I was at in my life's journey, what I had achieved and not achieved and also and more importantly what was important to me.

Of course family is the priority, nothing beats that, but as a music teacher for 40 years, music obviously is a huge priority in my life and always has been! Just ask my family! My siblings used to complain about how "noisy" I was, either practising one instrument or another or having the radio or stereo blasting! Mind you my siblings were all pretty good at getting their stereos blasting too, particularly when I was trying to concentrate on practise!

I take my music with me everywhere. With the amazing stuff technology allows us to do now, I always have my listening library in my pocket so if I'm stuck anywhere, or need some "quiet" time, I can pop on my headphones and chill out, or energise myself while I exercise, and listen to my favourite music to help me sleep when I am travelling. I'm sure

you know what I mean. Music is my "go to" thing for keeping me functioning at my best!

So after this small tussle with "the Big C", I guess I became a little introspective and started assessing things I was spending time on.

I am currently still teaching over 20 piano students individually each week, many of whom I have had for years. One of the most wonderful things of being a teacher is seeing students growing up, getting comfortable with you and letting you into their lives by sharing their dreams and goals, their ups and downs in life not just in music. I've often said that being a private music teacher is as much about being a psychologist, and a confidant, as it is about being a teacher and a musician all rolled into one person.

But what really struck me last year, was the IMPACT that music and music lessons can have in our students' lives.

We teach them to play some tunes or sing some songs and as part of that process we may teach them other musical knowledge, techniques etc, etc, but it's the experience of making music itself that has such huge impact, and that impact can be for anyone experiencing music – not just people learning to play or sing!

What do I mean by impact?

I mean the developing self-confidence of that super shy kid you started last year – the one who would never speak and who now bounds in the room telling you about their latest adventure.

I mean the adult who started from scratch and tells you with tears in their eyes that when they heard the recording of their latest piece, that it made

them cry to realise how good they sounded and that their adult daughters are also saying it too!!

I mean the proud parents and families cheering their child on no matter the mistakes just made at the end of term concert! The grandparent who comes specially to a lesson to thank you for helping their grandchild learn to play “Happy Birthday” for their special day.

I also mean those kids who have the creativity and confidence to get up and play an original song in front of their peers.

BUT and there is a BIG BUT!

As music teachers, I realised we (starting with me) can do so much more!

Music is made for sharing

AND

Music can benefit so many people who don’t have access to it.

Those with special needs
Those who are mentally or physically disabled
Those who are ill
Those who are old
Those who are very young
Those who have mental health issues
Those suffering high levels of stress
Those who are disengaged with society
Those who are financially disadvantaged
Those who are politically or culturally isolated and I’m sure you can think of others that could be added to this list!

So I'm on a mission.

A MUSIC MISSION

To spread music to more people who can benefit from it and get more music in communities.

You can join this growing global tribe on Facebook here... www.facebook.com/groups/musicmissiontribe/ and interact with like-minded musicians and teachers, therapists, composers and others passionate about music.

And as part of this mission, I am also giving and sharing my 40 years expertise in music education to musicians and music teachers to help them do what I am doing... becoming more and more aware of how we can use music to IMPACT more lives.

This book is part of that desire to "spread more music" by helping music teachers make sustainable careers, and enjoyable lives as this enables them to keep going and have continued and increasing impact. In this book I will share with you a number of strategies and systems I have developed over the many years of my teaching and business career.

Musicians and music teachers are often highly trained, and highly skilled in all things musical, however they are rarely as highly trained, if trained at all, in what it takes to run a business. When I was starting out, there was nothing available. In fact only recently has this changed as there appear to be opportunities now emerging for music teachers to learn and understand the business side of their teaching, but most of it is generic for any sort of business and I doubt you will find many music teacher mentors with 40 years hands on experience in the industry.

My goal is to help you find a clear and easy path to success and a sustainable and profitable music school, or music teaching business by sharing what I had to learn the hard way, through trial and error, horrendously long hours and bad decisions, so you can avoid those things.

Don't let anyone tell you it is easy to build a music school that achieves a great lifestyle and high income. It takes dedication and persistence and business knowledge, being a great muso or a great teacher just won't be enough.

How to use this book:

Athletes, actors, musicians and sports people use coaches to improve their skill, their knowledge, their technique and to be made accountable. Ultimately they need someone who can see the "bigger picture", someone who has been where they are and can help avoid pitfalls, and plan steps forward to enable them to achieve their dreams and goals in the quickest and most effective way.

This book will share with you a small amount of my experiences on my own personal journey building, growing and expanding my music schools in their various formats.

For those of you who are serious about also developing their music teaching into a successful and profitable career as well as a rewarding one, then this book will not be enough.

On my website www.WendysMusic.com.au under the "For teachers" menu, you will find a much more extensive list of resources and coaching options as well as free stuff to help you achieve what you want.

This book aims to give you a taste of the systems and strategies and also some examples of the phases of development building a music school or music teaching business goes through, the business divisions that are the pillars that support it and the levels of the Music School Success Ladder to which you can aspire.

I will share with you what I experienced at each level of the Music School Success Ladder and you will discover some of the pitfalls to avoid along the way based on my own experience and that of the music teachers I have been privileged to know and work with along the way.

I hope you get some great learning from this book and that you can enjoy your journey as a music teacher. I also hope to meet you in my MUSIC MISSION Facebook group or via my website www.WendysMusic.com.au where you can find further resources to take you beyond where one book can go.

Yours musically
Wendy

CHAPTER 2

OVERVIEW

Before I start to share my Music School career journey and strategies with you, I would like to explain three key systems I developed as my business grew, as these will be referred to throughout the book.

Like many music teachers I started my "business" by teaching from home or in student's homes. I didn't actually consider that I was running a "business" — it was a way of earning money, but not a "proper" business! As time went on and my students and income grew, I found that operating as a solo teacher was quite different to operating with admin staff, teachers and growing numbers of students, families and schools. I had to learn how to run a "real" business! I spent a lot of time figuring out what worked and didn't work for a music school, often through trial and error, and it's definitely true that you learn a lot from making mistakes! I know from having had lots of experience at making mistakes as well as success! These "trial and error" and other experiences led over time to the development of the three systems.

The systems are known as the:

1. Music School Success Evolution
2. Music School Success Ladder
3. Music School Success Divisions

Identifying the phases of development a business must undertake for growth was a key component to knowing what steps to undertake for each expansion phase of my music school business. So at each stage of my business, such as moving from being a solo teacher to employing teachers to work with me OR opening a second, third or fourth retail studio, I had a clear set of steps to follow and realistic expectations.

This is known as the around "Music School Success Evolution" system

As my business grew I also discovered the importance of sharing my vision of growth with my team of staff and teachers. This meant being able to articulate where we were currently in terms of business structure, size, resources and requirements and also what I wanted the business to grow into. This required clarity of each part of the business in order to plan adequately for the future growth, its impact upon staff, resources and so forth. Essentially identifying a clear system of Business Growth by size and structure.

This is the around "Music School Success Ladder" system

When you train your first member of staff, even in a role you have been doing yourself, perhaps for years, you find out very quickly how organised (or not!) that role is! Do you have systems for every procedure? Are they documented? Are they efficient? As a solo teacher you are a jack of all trades. As your business grows, you will want to have staff or consultants or contractors taking over tasks that you don't enjoy or aren't good at so you can concentrate on what you get most satisfaction and best results from. I discovered a little late in my journey, the value of defining roles, tasks and of documenting and systemising everything.

This is known as the Music School Success Divisions system

The Seven Stages of evolution or development to create a profitable Music School.

1. Prepare — working out what resources you already have
2. Dream — deep thinking to unveil your deepest desires (music related!)
3. Design — planning how to turn the dreams into reality
4. Build — doing the work to bring the plans to life
5. Live — testing and tweaking time
6. Share — making an impact with your music school
7. Expand — growing in size, responsibility and income

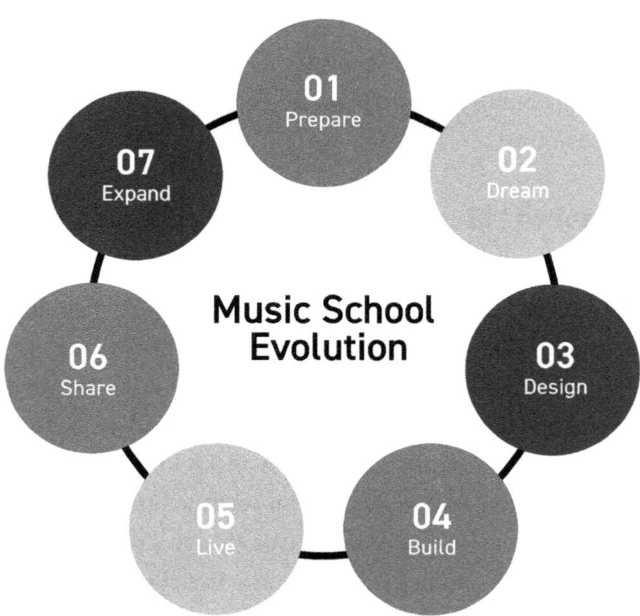

The Nine Steps of the Music School Success Ladder are:

FOUNDATION STAGE

1. The Roadie — not yet teaching
2. The Chorus Line — teaching mostly for someone else
3. The One Person Show — teaching mostly for yourself

ENTERPRISE STAGE

4. The Leading Person — teaching for yourself with a small number of staff teachers
5. The Principal — teaching around 50% of your time, with a number of staff teachers
6. The Manager — 100% of your time on admin and business with growing number of teachers

ALCHEMY STAGE

7. The Director — multiple locations and manager assistance
8. The Virtuosos — removed from management, multiple businesses like a franchise
9. The Icon — sought after, with multiple income streams

PRINCIPLES OF THE MUSIC SCHOOL SUCCESS LADDER

1. Everyone has a position on the Ladder.
   Whether you are a musician trying to start teaching or a Master Teacher who has little or no teaching, everyone fits within a step.
2. There is always someone at every step of the ladder.
   Every step has an economic role and every person has different needs, goals and skills, meaning there is always someone at each step of the ladder.
3. The Ladder is your map to success.
   We change stages and steps as we go through our life. Understanding the Nine Steps, where you are and how to move up and down steps empowers you to build a path to your own success.
4. The step you are on determines your reality.
   Every step has different skill sets and demands. When we move steps we need to change our focus and awareness and develop or extend new skills. The problems and opportunities will vary at each step.
5. The step you are on is your choice.
   When you know your step, it is your choice to stay at that step, move up or move down. Each step has benefits and disadvantages. Knowing your step gives you the power to focus yourself on moving to where you want to be. It is your choice.

The Eight Business Divisions or Management Areas are;

1. **Finance**
   a. It's all about the money = Banking
   b. Income and expense reporting
   c. Payment systems
2. **Intellectual Property (IP)**
   a. Your musical creations
   b. Your programs
   c. Your business systems
3. **Legal**
   a. Contracts
   b. Leases
   c. Policy documents
4. **Merchandise (Merch)**
   a. Anything you sell, books, programs, instruments etc.
5. **Operations (Ops)**
   a. Administration processes
   b. Systems that make things work
6. **Human Resources (HR)**
   a. Your staff
   b. Consultants
   c. Freelancers
7. **Information technology (IT)**
   a. Everything tech related
8. **Marketing**
   a. Paid Advertising
   b. Unpaid advertising
   c. Public Relations (PR)

The three systems can all be at play concurrently — meaning you can be working on developing a particular division of your business at a particular time of your business evolution to achieve a particular expansion or growth in your teaching business.

So now that you have an overview of my three systems, it's time to take you on a journey of how I created my Profitable Music Schools in a variety of different formats using these systems.

Along the way you will also find out pitfalls to avoid and strategies to assist with the most common problems music teachers encounter.

Enjoy!

PART 2

THE EVOLUTION OF A MUSIC SCHOOL

CHAPTER 3

PREPARE

So if you are thinking that you want to make music teaching into a career where you are independent and have the freedom to choose when, where, what and who you teach then you might be asking…

Where do I start?

You might though be reading this and already getting ready to flip to the next chapter because you have already started teaching, have a handful of students and are therefore beyond this level? I urge you to STOP – don't flip the page and bear with me, as every stage has some value to everyone. It only takes one golden nugget to transform your mind and change your approach, and I hope to give you at least one of those on your journey through this book. To get a bucketful of nuggets you might consider more extensive coaching as can be found on my website www.WendysMusic.com.au under the Music School Success Coaching Brand.

So if you are already teaching a little and want to grow, or if you are teaching a lot and want to scale up to employing teachers or expand to multiple locations, then you still need to consider each phase of development.

Why? I'm not just trying to be pedantic! (I have a few pedantic family members and know what that can be like to live with!) It's a process that means you are covering all the bases, you are crossing all the "t's" and dotting all the i's and will therefore get the best value from the time, energy and money that you put into the development.

PREPARE! This is the first step of the Music School Success Evolution system.

Step 1: Prepare Yourself!

To get the best of the process of developing your music teaching business though, your mind needs to be OPEN to change. You should be prepared to use your imagination and try on different ideas. Ask yourself questions like: “What would it look like/feel like and so on if I tried this, changed that and so on…

If you find yourself reacting to ideas or strategies with thoughts like:

- That wouldn’t work for me!
- I shouldn’t need to do that!
- I don’t feel comfortable doing that.
- Why should I?
- I’ve never done it that way before.
- I don’t know anyone who is doing that!

I strongly urge, encourage and persuade you to acknowledge those thoughts, then put them aside and try the idea on for size. Turn the thoughts around by asking yourself questions like:

- Why wouldn’t it work for me?
- Why shouldn’t I do it?
- Why wouldn’t I feel comfortable?
- Why shouldn’t I?
- What have I got to lose changing things up?
- Does it matter if I don’t know anyone else doing it?

Once you have agreed to be open minded, ready to change and try new things, only then are you ready to actually get started at developing your music teaching business.

Step 2: Prepare your resources.

This stage is all about preparing the resources you already have, and therefore knowing if you have limitations or open ended resources.

As you might recall from the overview chapter, I have a system of Eight Business Divisions that you will hear me refer to repeatedly from here on. Let's start using them now to do your Resource Audit.

Let's go through each Business Division and make a list of what resources you have available. The following will give you a starting point, if not a conclusive list.

For those of you who may choose to get personalised coaching, or subscribe to one of my online courses, you will find detailed templates available for action steps such as this Audit.

FINANCE

Do you know how much money you have available to fund your business? Time to audit your finances.
Do you have a financial budget or plan?
What online banking services do you use?

IP

Do you have any unique teaching materials, programs, packages, workshops or such?
Have you got a business logo?

LEGAL

What bank accounts do you have?
Do you have business insurance?
What registrations do you have?
Are you operating under a particular business structure? Partnership? Company etc.?
Do you own your business and domain name?

MERCHANDISE

What saleable stock do you have currently?

OPERATIONS

What instruments, equipment and teaching materials do you currently have available to use?
What location do you have, or plan to have available to use?
How much time do you have to put into this project?

HUMAN RESOURCES

What network of consultants, friends and supporters do you have who can help you?

INFORMATION TECHNOLOGY (IT)

What devices, software and systems do you currently have set up or access to?

MARKETING

Do you have website, social media profiles, online presence and a unique brand?

This list may appear extensive, but a lot of it can be done quite quickly initially, however it's then also worth putting some careful thought into it, as it will be your guideline for future steps along the journey. My recommendation is that you set aside an hour or so to get started, then "mull over" the requirements and see if you can think creatively about alternatively resources that might be possible.

PREPARE – ACTION STEPS

Before you move to the next chapter, make a list of all your resources, in the Eight Business Divisions, starting with the list above.

Keep it handy then as you read through further chapters.

Once done, it's time to congratulate you on taking this first step!

You are ready to move to Stage 2 – DREAM!

CHAPTER 4

DREAM

Do you know your why?

Do you know what level you are on the MSS ladder

Do you know what level what you to get to on the MSS ladder?

Do you know your strengths and weaknesses?

Values and Mission Statement?

Do you have a clear picture of what you want your business and your life to look like in the future?

So if you took action from the last chapter, you would now have done an audit of your resources in readiness for taking further action towards creating your profitable music teaching business or music school.

Next comes what I consider the FUN part!

Now this may come easily to some of you, whilst others will find it takes effort to get into the flow of it, but ultimately the more you can let go of any limiting beliefs and ideas about what you should be doing, or what other people have told you that you should do, the easier it becomes.

This is the time when I want your creativity to RUN RIOT! So let's get started.

So you want to start a Music School/Music Studio? Why?

- Is it because you just love making music yourself?
- You want to be in a job where you are surrounded by music all day?
- Perhaps it's because somebody has told you that you would be good at it?
- Would it be because you need a part-time or even full-time job and thought this was a way of using your musical skills?
- Maybe it's just for the money! You think the hourly rate of music teachers earn is more than you'll get in retail or hospitality or other jobs.
- Or is it that you really love helping others learn and grow and music is important to you?
- Is it because you can get lots of holiday times if you teach school kids?

There are many reasons why people start teaching music to others, and everyone of course is motivated differently and comes to it at different times in their life.

Being a Private Music Teacher, running your own music school has a lot of advantages!

1. Flexible hours — you choose when and how much to teach.
2. You make ALL the decisions.
3. Take holidays when it suits you.
4. Enables you to work from home.
5. The hourly rate is often better than many other part-time jobs.
6. You get to be surrounded by music all day!

For me, becoming a music teacher was my only career plan.

Music was and still is my passion.

I use music in many aspects of my life and I want to share the joy and benefits I have received from music with as many people as possible.

I was one of the kids that started out singing under the kitchen table as a toddler, then in primary school was in the recorder group and choir and in high school tried every music ensemble and learnt multiple instruments! I was also the only one of the four kids in my house who begged to learn piano at age eight and stuck at it through uni!

At the time I was due to start university, the normal courses for music were only teaching or performing with Music Therapy just beginning as an unknown factor the year I began at Melbourne University Conservatorium. So for me the choice was a Performance course or a Teaching course. I knew I didn't have the temperament for performing as a career so it was a no-brainer…teaching!

I even started teaching piano to support myself financially as I went through uni, and continued teaching privately even after I started full time in the classroom. When I married and started a family, the classroom teaching had to go, but the private teaching continued – in fact I was back teaching only eight weeks after each of my children were born! And I had three!

As my teaching career progressed I became driven by the need to provide a better quality teaching program across multiple instruments, not just my major instrument, piano.

Whilst teaching every other instrument, I had found the lack of supplementary material such as Theory, Sight Reading and Improvisation for violin, guitar and woodwinds, to be very limiting for my students and made my job teaching them a comprehensive approach so much harder.

So I created my own Teaching Method for seven instruments.

And so on it went, I was continually striving to make better experiences, simpler programs and to train other teachers to use them.

So eventually I articulated my WHY as

> *"I am passionate about encouraging and inspiring people to begin to experience the heart filling joy of making music in a simple, easy and systematic way, enabling them to enrich their lives and the lives of those around them."*

It's OK though to change and update your WHY… as I have done since my cancer episode.

What is your WHY?
What gives you energy, makes you wake up every day wanting more?
What inspires you to want to run a music school?
It's about WHAT we do, HOW we do it and WHY we do it.
Your WHY is your Passion, your inspiration
What gives you Purpose, what is your Belief, your Cause?

When we discover our WHY we are better able to find clarity and confidence to make choices and connect with a network of people and communities that inspire us.

We are also better able to communicate with the rest of the world about what we do.

When we discover our WHY we no longer live by accident, we can be fulfilled by living on purpose, living deliberately.

What does your DREAM Music School look like? What is your Future Vision?

When I first started out as qualified music teacher, my dream was to become the Head of Music at a school. Plans changed however once I had a family, but not in the way you might think!

As I mentioned earlier in this course, I started teaching as a uni student, and I saw no reason to stop when I graduated and started teaching full time classroom. (Oh the energy of youth!) I really enjoyed the private lessons I was giving from home and had many loyal students.

It wasn't long before I was married and having my own kids, which meant I gave up my classroom teaching and focussed totally on private lessons from my own home.

I found that I was in such demand that I took on some casual teachers to help me and it grew from there, to being invited to teach at the schools of my students and so on… It actually wasn't something I dreamed of at the start, but I certainly wasn't unhappy about it.

Having my own kids at school also meant further demand for my services.

We ended up running approximately 30 primary school programs around Melbourne when we decided to franchise the business.

It was a later decision to go into afterschool programs in retail studios and now a further development is in the pipeline for teachers to become Certified to teach our method from their own homes.

In so many ways, my original dream of being Head of Music at a school is not dissimilar to being Head of my own private music school, however my advice to you is that Dreaming, then Planning and Taking Action will certainly make your life easier and more predictable!

You've had a glimpse of what it looks like at each level of the MSS Ladder, and perhaps you have done some research or have an existing music school in mind that you aspire to be like – either way it's time to document your dreams as the first step to making them happen.

It doesn't matter where you are currently located on the Music School Success Ladder.

What matters is having a Dream and building a Vision that can ultimately become a plan of action to get you there.

Do you day dream about opening your own music school and imagine a building with multiple studios, sounds of many instruments pouring out? Do you imagine queues of students coming and going, exciting concert performances, with happy smiling faces?

Perhaps you prefer to daydream about having a dedicated room in your house set up with all the instruments and equipment you ever wished for, and a steady stream of children coming after school for individual lessons?

No matter what your dream is, it is important to HAVE a dream, as without a dream, nothing will change.

ACTION STEP 1 – RESEARCH

Many of you may already have ideas on what sort of music teaching business you want to build or grow BUT (there's always one isn't there!), even if you think you have clear ideas, I believe it's worth doing some exploratory research to see what others are doing.

Why research others?

Firstly it's always good to see what your competition are doing so you can see that there is a demand in your area.

Secondly you might see that they are missing an opportunity that you could capitalise on – for example, perhaps they don't teach preschoolers? Or perhaps they don't offer exams, or ensembles or whatever is your "thing"… that means you can make that a prominent part of what you do and attract students that would otherwise have missed out!

Thirdly they may have ideas of programs or classes that you are skilled in but never thought to offer – in which case you would have been missing out on potential students without realising it!

ACTION STEP 2 – DOCUMENT

Work through each of the Eight Business Divisions and using as many SPECIFICS as possible, document a description of what you would like you music school and your life to look like in 12 months' time.

FINANCE

What revenue would you like to raise? And how much will be your personal income? Put aside as superannuation or investment?

IP

What teaching classes types, instruments, programs, workshops other activities will you offer?

LEGAL

What business structure would you like to have? A sole trader/one person show or more like a large company with multiple staff and teachers?

MERCHANDISE

Will you offer products other than teaching? If so what?

OPERATIONS

How would you like your music business to operate? Do your ideas of systems you would like to build or at least how things get done? Do you want to manage everything to do with teaching but have someone/ something else do all the administration?

HUMAN RESOURCES

What staff would your Dream Business have? Admin? Marketing?

How many teachers would you like?

INFORMATION TECHNOLOGY (IT)

What would your Dream Technology systems look like?

What devices, software or tasks would technology do for you?

MARKETING

What sort of targets would you aspire to? How many students enrol each month? term? year?

What other sales would you be aiming for?

Add this "Future Vision" Document to your Folder with your "Resources Checklist".

It's also a good idea to print a copy and put on the wall somewhere where you will see it often – that could be on your fridge, beside your desk or bed or even the toilet door! Your choice!

In sight means in front of mind.

Keep referring to it as you read through further chapters.

Once again if you're done, it's time to congratulate you on taking this SECOND step closer to your Dream Life.

You are ready to move to Stage 3 – DESIGN!

CHAPTER 5

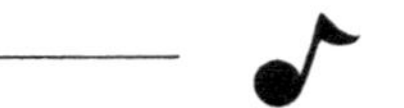

DESIGN

You've made it!

I've got my fingers crossed that this means you have now actually visualised what your dream music teaching business or music school actually looks like!

I'm also hoping that you are now getting really excited at all the potential of how you can change your life! Of course there is the potential for fear and overwhelm to join the party, so perhaps now is a good time to let you into some of the secrets of running a professional business.

1. It can be scary
2. It can be hard work
3. It takes focus
4. It takes determination

IT IS SO WORTH IT!

So if at any time in this journey you are tempted to stop taking action, or if you are overwhelmed with the volume of stuff to do or decisions to make, then I would love you to reach out to me and have a conversation. Sometimes you just need to be able to talk to someone who understands what you are trying to do, why you are doing it without judgment and perhaps to share some insights too!

I'm easy to find to, so you can jump on Facebook and search for "Wendy Brentnall" – there's not many of us! and as far as I know I'm the only crazy music coach with that name!

DREAM to DESIGN…How do we do this?

The Design stage is very much a research stage.

You take your ideas and dreams and figure out HOW to make them real.

So you take what you want to achieve and choose what resources and systems, staff or products you feel suit you best. Easy right?

So let's take a look at those Eight Business Divisions again and see what things you might need to research.

FINANCE

1. What financial software, bank accounts, business credit card (online and offline) will you need? Talking to your accountant if you have one is a great idea at this time! He/she may have a clear idea of what will work best for the size of your business and to coordinate with them.
2. Research what lesson fees you can and wish to charge.

IP

1. Research is needed before you go too far, on what business name, logos, domain, program names and trademarks are available for use.
2. In additional you want to design your programs in more depth – who, what and when will you teach? with what resources?

LEGAL

1. Research what registrations, permits, insurance and so forth are needed for your location.
2. Consider business, instrument, public liability or professional indemnity insurances, however don't feel obliged to rush into everything at once!
3. Very importantly research what lesson policies and other policies are going to work for the life and business you want to create. Consider using a professional to assist in the actual wording of these documents to ensure you are compliant and covered.

MERCHANDISE

1. What products would you like to offer? Instruments? Equipment? Books? Other things??
2. Research what sales systems are suitable to you.
3. Research what hire systems you could use.

OPERATIONS

1. Have you done the research of your location yet? If you are looking for a retail premises you had better get cracking then!
2. If you are planning to work from home then now is the time to design your space.
3. It's also time to design your administration, communication, enquiry and enrolment systems

INFORMATION TECHNOLOGY (IT)

1. Hardware, Software, Internet, Email, Website, Security – you'll need it all! Research any of the areas that you have gaps or need to expand.

HUMAN RESOURCES

1. Do you know what costs are involved in employing and recruiting staff and teachers? If not research now so you know what you'll need.
2. If you're not employing staff then it's time to research the best superannuation offer for yourself and also what is the most cost effective way for you to get paid by your business.

MARKETING

1. At this time, you should put as much energy as you can into designing your BRAND.
2. Based on your Why and your Values and IP that you have already defined, you should be feeling confident enough to start crafting what your marketing message is going to be and start writing some descriptions of what you are offering, who you are and so forth.
3. You can then start designing (hopefully with some professional help) your Brand and styling.
   It's also worth researching that your Social handles are available for your prospective business name too!
4. Lastly consider what sort of Marketing you want to start with and research costs and timelines!
5. I would focus first on designing a "PRE LAUNCH Marketing Campaign" that can start prior to doors opening and get you off to a flying start. I'm sure you've seen advertising saying "Coming Soon"… "Enrol for next term"…
6. If possible then design your "ongoing" marketing campaign also, based on your research and budget. Be prepared to "tweak" it as you discover what works for you and what doesn't.

ACTION STEP

Document all your research and ideas into a document or folder and add this Research Document to your other documents.

Once again if you're done, it's time to congratulate you on taking this THIRD step closer to your Dream Life.

You are ready to move to Stage 4 – BUILD IT! This is the serious stuff now!

CHAPTER 6

BUILD

You should now be at a stage where you know what you want, you've done your big picture dreaming and followed it with some research to see how you can achieve it. The Building Stage is all about taking action and setting up your business so that it will be efficient, professional and enjoyable from your very first transaction.

It's where your business actually gets set up and becomes a reality!

So if you haven't taken the ACTION STEPS of the previous chapters, I strongly suggest you stop reading and go back to them. Planning and research now can save you a lot of grief in the future!

As you get going though, if you have doubts or feel you need someone to help motivate you to keep going, then remember to jump on Facebook find and connect with me "Wendy Brentnall" if you need some help!

DESIGN to BUILD…How do we do this?

The Building Stage is where things get VERY, VERY real.

In this stage you will be required to "Put your money where your mouth/ ideas are" and spend some money. It could be on equipment, software, registrations, equipment or even premises and marketing. The amount

and timing of what you spend very much depends on your dreams, goals as well as your budget – it's your call.

As always there will be great variation in how long this stage may take you to complete. You may have already started some of these steps whilst you were researching, and if so well done for taking the plunge!

If you are moving into a retail premises or building a website, then be prepared for those things to take a considerable amount of time as they most likely will be dependent upon people other than yourself and quite possibly involve several layers of work to be done.

So let's take a look at what you might need to set up in each of the Eight Business Divisions.

FINANCE

1. Purchase your subscription to a financial software program.
   - set up account lists
   - set up opening balances
2. Open your business bank account (NB often you need to have your business name registered first)
3. Open your business credit card.
4. Document all your lesson fees for future reference.

IP

1. Register your business name with your state or government authority.
2. Register your domain name, purchase a hosting account for your website.
3. Document all your program names.

4. If you are at a point where trademarks are recommended then register those either through a trademarks lawyer or registered government body.
5. Employ a designer to bring your logo to life.
6. Bring your programs to life by creating the lessons, modules, packages and their content to some degree. This will most likely be an ongoing process whilst you test and tweak how they work with actual students once you start using them, so it's not necessary to have finished products just yet.

LEGAL

1. Submit registration and permit applications as required.
2. Purchase relevant business, Work cover, instrument, public liability or professional indemnity insurance as needed for your location.
3. Complete your lesson policy document suitable for giving students and for your website.
4. If relevant complete other policy documents for staff and employees.

MERCHANDISE

1. Complete applications to your preferred suppliers of instruments, music, equipment.
2. Document your hire prices and policies if applicable.
3. Document your sales systems.
4. If using an online sales portal, then complete the set-up and load the necessary product information.

OPERATIONS

1. If renting or purchasing a retail premises, it's well and truly time to sign your lease, pick up the keys and do the necessary fit out for your retail studio(s) (Allow weeks for this).
2. Measure up and order your furniture.
3. Measure up and have your external signage constructed. (This may take several weeks).
4. Order and arrange your teaching instruments and equipment.
5. Organise your merchandise display.
6. Set up your chosen administration software or systems.
7. Document your enquiry and enrolment systems – prepare any forms.
8. SET AN OPENING DATE!

HUMAN RESOURCES

1. Document staff employment procedures.
2. Prepare staff employment forms and folders.
3. Set up your superannuation account.
4. Set up any tax forms or documentation.

INFORMATION TECHNOLOGY (IT)

1. Set up your computer hardware, software.
2. Internet, email.
3. Website.
4. Security across all your devices.

MARKETING

1. Complete writing descriptions of all the lessons and programs you offer, remembering to differentiate yourself. If possible write several versions – suitable for using in ads but also in dot point form suitable to discuss with new enquiries.
2. Write a short bio of yourself and make sure you have some professional photos of yourself and your studio taken.
3. Set up your chosen social media profiles and start posting and engaging here.
4. Find a website developer and start building your web presence (this will take weeks or months)
5. Using your program descriptions and bio and photos, list your studio on as many online music teaching websites as you can. NB Some are free, some are paid only, and some you have the choice. To stand out more quickly, it can be worthwhile having a paid listing.
6. Based on your research you should now put into action your PRE-LAUNCH marketing campaign for your music school. Launching your marketing prior to opening your doors is essential if you have rent and costs of a retail premises. You need to start earning asap!

ACTION STEP

By now you should have done all the action needed for this stage of business development.

Once again if you have completed as much as you can here, it's time to congratulate yourself on taking this FOURTH step closer to your Dream Life.

You are ready to move to Stage 5 – time to LIVE the Dream!

CHAPTER 7

LIVE IT!

If you have been taking action as you move through this book, then you should now be at the stage of LAUNCHING your business.

You will have set in motion your Pre-Launch Marketing Plan and started taking enquiries and bookings and your OPENING DATE has arrived!

Regardless whether you are opening a retail premises or working from your own home, both scenarios should be treated as professional endeavours with the same launch procedure.

In the previous stage of your business evolution, you set up each business division, and now you actually get to see, hear, feel and experience whether the systems you've envisaged and put together and the programs you've dreamed of, actually work as you expected them to.

This stage is one of testing, reviewing and tweaking and then repeat the sequence as much as needed!

TEST
REVIEW
TWEAK
REPEAT

The stage is almost experimental, with trial and error seen as a viable means of determining the best outcome.

Of course if you have a coach or mentor who can guide you in your choices of dreaming, designing and building your music school, then the chances of needing to test and try systems, policies, and so forth is greatly reduced. This is where the benefit of someone else's experience is invaluable as it can save you a lot of time and therefore a lot of energy and potentially also a lot of money.

So if you are in fact feeling a little lost or overwhelmed with what will achieve your dreams most effectively, or what systems you should prioritise or such, then I suggest you invest your money and time first in professional advice from someone who has done what you want to do. Not just a business coach as they won't understand your type of business, but a Music Teacher's coach or mentor… someone like me in fact!

Check out my website www.WendysMusic.com.au for the latest online courses and coaching programs designed specifically to help people like you in a much more in depth way than a book can.

At this point in your journey, don't be afraid to get feedback from your "customers" either! You can do this in a formal way by setting up surveys that are sent out as part of your enrolment or continuity program, or more casually by having casual but deliberate conversations with students and or parents of students.

It's also worth noting any potential student enquiry feedback you get. Keeping a log of communications and tracking conversions and comments on a simple spreadsheet or phone log system can be a simple way to start. Just remember to refer to it to help you make decisions.

This business evolution phase is very variable in how long it will last. Some people can achieve answers quickly – meaning they have been able to review all their systems and results and be confident in the choices they have made even with some tweaks. They may also be happy with the growth achieved quickly, dependent upon the effectiveness of their marketing campaign.

So it may be a matter of months or it could be a year or more for others as they try out a variety of teaching programs, marketing ideas and so forth. There is no definitively correct length of time for "living" with your business and getting it to run at its most efficient and effective. In fact it should be a life-long goal of a business owner to keep reviewing and updating.

So let's take a look at what you might need to Test and Tweak in each of the Eight Business Divisions during this stage.

FINANCE

1. Is your financial software set up correctly i.e. accounts list, GST, etc.
2. Can you easily produce profit and loss statements with enough detail to know how your income and all your expenses are tracking?

IP

1. Are you making tweaks and adding new ideas to your programs and lessons based on student and potential student feedback?

LEGAL

1. Are your lesson policies working for you? Do you need to add or change any?
2. Other policy documents?

MERCHANDISE

1. What products are your students asking for or needing? Do you have suppliers?
2. Are your sales and/or hire systems working effectively?
3. Are you making any sales? Or hires?

OPERATIONS

1. Is the layout of your teaching space(s) working well?
2. Is the signage having an effect?
3. Is your equipment meeting all your needs?
4. Is your administration systems running smoothly?
5. Is your enquiry and enrolment systems working well?

HUMAN RESOURCES

1. Are all staff procedures doing what they should efficiently?

INFORMATION TECHNOLOGY (IT)

1. Is all your IT working for you? Do you need to add or change any?

MARKETING

1. How is Social Media engagement? Any enquiries?
2. How are your website stats?
3. What response are you getting from online directories?
4. What response did your PRE-LAUNCH Marketing Campaign bring?
5. What ongoing marketing are you doing?

ACTION STEP

As listed above there needs to be a review of each facet of your business now for this stage of business development and in the future as a regular occurrence.

The above list is not necessarily conclusive either, but I'm sure you get the point that you need to experience the reality of how things work in your business and be prepared to make changes if things either aren't working or if you feel they could be more efficient or effective.

Avoid the "shiny object syndrome" though where you keep changing and chasing after the latest shiny object or latest software or app or program and not allow anything to settle in and show its true value.

Whilst congratulating yourself on getting to the stage of LIVING your dream, you are also ready to move to Stage 6 – time to SHARE the Dream!

The SHARING stage can work concurrently with this LIVING stage, as it is where you, your music school and your students start to take music into your community and have a tangible and positive impact on spreading the benefits of music.

CHAPTER 8

SHARE IT!

Music is made for Sharing.

You've heard that before I'm sure!

As musicians we have an awesome opportunity to do a lot of good in our community whilst also gaining respect and authority as the local expert.

The more you are seen out and about in your community doing musical things, the more people will remember you as the local muso and the more referrals you will get – it's a fact.

Taking yourself and your students or musician friends out to share music in the community also shows you as a person who cares about others and is passionate about music.

Why wouldn't people want to come to you to learn?

But how?

I like to think of SHARING in two ways.

1. **SHARING MUSIC with YOUR STUDENTS,**
   i.e. sharing with them music that is relevant to them.

AND

2. SHARING MUSIC with YOUR COMMUNITY
i.e. by making music with and for other people in your community.

Let's start by looking at…

1. SHARING MUSIC with YOUR STUDENTS

It's an unfortunate fact that over time with changes to lifestyle through the industrial revolution and the age of technology (and other changes), the role of music in people's lives has changed. Music used to be a way of passing on stories through folk song, and as entertainment in pubs and private halls, gatherings as well as part of religious celebration and rituals and so much more.

Today's students sometimes only get to perform in the bedroom or lounge room. Some students don't get to choose the music they play, its either dictated by teachers, parents, schools or exam institutions. The result is often boredom or frustration and ultimately a loss of motivation to continue learning. We all know that learning to play an instrument (and I include singing here) takes dedication. It's not something that most people can pick up and do within a few weeks at an advanced level.

What I'm suggesting is that when we share music with our students, we make it relevant to them by:
- taking into account the music they enjoy.
- taking into account the musical activities they want to participate in (jamming with friends, garage band, choir, open mic sessions, family events, eisteddfods or whatever).

It's important to understand that I don't mean we allow the students to dictate what they should learn entirely, as that would be downright silly – as professional educators they should recognise our wisdom in knowing what is important for them to learn, but you can cater to their preferences within those parameters, if not with every piece of music or activity, but with enough for them to see the progress and feel the stimulation of achieving some of the goals they have.

You might be thinking that that all sounds good for intermediate or advanced students, but what about beginners? There's so much they need to learn before they can play much right? Sure, but at the same time they can learn to play some simple things like Christmas carols or other celebratory music, football themes and even "Happy Birthday"!

Being able to play music that they and their family recognise and that can be used within their daily life will give them confidence, and their family will also see greater value in these outcomes from their lessons and yes that can mean greater student retention too!

So it's a win for all involved!

2. SHARING MUSIC with YOUR COMMUNITY

What activities could you do?

1. Performance
   - Informal and formal performance opportunities. Participants could be local ensembles, amateur musicians or music students
2. Lessons
   - Lessons offered by music teachers and music schools
3. Ensembles
   - Contact local orchestras, choirs, bands and other music ensembles for opportunities for recipients to experience what it is like to be part of an ensemble
4. Teaching workshops BY teachers
   - Sessions taken by teachers or "specialist musicians"
5. Jam session
   - Workshop/jam sessions – invite local ADULT musos and music students, (amateurs and pros) to bring some basic gear in and play and lead jam sessions on a mix of instruments including hand percussion and karaoke type trax (for the non-musos) or drum circles or singalong/karaoke sessions.
6. Therapy sessions
   - Sessions led by a teacher or therapist or experienced amateur
7. Competitions
   - Competitions online or at local community festivals or markets

Who could you share with for greatest impact?

1. Disengaged youth
2. Elderly
3. Kinders and childcare
4. Hospitals
5. Prisons
6. Unemployed
7. Special needs
8. Remote communities
9. Low income/disadvantaged schools
10. Local communities
11. Refugees
12. Mental Health Institutions

ACTION STEP

1. Decide on which of the suggested activities and people that suit you and your music school to share with.
2. Contact the relevant organisations to make it happen.
3. Put dates on your calendar to make things happen.
4. Promote within your school.

Whilst still working through Stage 5 – LIVING your Dream Business, AND sharing it with your community, you can begin to consider the last stage which is Stage 7 EXPAND.

These final three stages can all be developed concurrently, in fact I encourage you to think and plan in advance, which means exploring the EXPAND stage before you are ready for it and deciding if it's what you want. There is also the decision of HOW BIG you want to expand to as seen if you refer back to the Music School Success Ladder.

Congratulations on getting through Stage 6 and onwards to Stage 7 – EXPAND!

CHAPTER 9

EXPAND

A profitable music teaching business can be different for different people largely based on what their ideal level on the Music School Success Ladder is.

For example, someone at Level 3 on the MSS ladder – the One Person Show – may be very happy to achieve the equivalent of a full time wage and call that "profitable".

As you climb higher up the ladder to Level 6 – the Manager's level, there is more likely to be an expectation of achieving a "profit" that far exceeds an average full-time wage as reward for the additional responsibilities, time, energy and commitment being a manager entails.

Within the MSS levels there will also be personal variations of what "profitable" means from an exact dollar figure.

The most simplistic view would be that as your Music Teaching Business grows in its number of teachers, staff and locations i.e. as you EXPAND your Music Teaching Business, then your profitability will increase meaning you can earn MORE through expanding.

When is a good time to expand?

Some teachers start to think of expanding when:

1. Their studio is completely or almost completely booked.
2. They can see potential to earn more at the next level.
3. When an opportunity such as a local teacher retiring or moving offering their student list occurs.
4. They feel they are teaching more than they would like to.
5. They have students requesting to learn a second instrument they can't personally offer.

The Reality?

Anytime is a good time to expand IF you have the resources and commitment to do so with the necessary thought and planning.

CASE STUDY

One of my coaching clients Lauren, contacted me as she was keen to begin expanding her studio from being a solo teacher to employing her first teacher.

Lauren kept steady student numbers for her own teaching and had started to build a waiting list of students referred to her by her own students. Problem was she found students wouldn't stay on her waiting list long before they got tired of waiting and went elsewhere.

Lauren was keen to find a teacher who could teach in her house as she had a spare room that she could easily convert to a second teaching room without breaking any council regulations and without paying rent. She felt that having students coming to her home would also give her greater ability to monitor every aspect of the lessons being given by the other teacher.

As part of her coaching sessions, Lauren and I worked through the following tasks.

Tasks:

1. Audit current resources and resources the second teaching room requires for use by a second teacher. (music books, instruments, computer, metronome, stationery, etc.)
2. Create a Teacher Recruitment Process (job description, interview template, contract, marketing).
3. Create Student Recruitment, Enquiry, Enrolment procedures suited to a second teacher (potentially different/altered procedures to when she teaches a student).
4. Start marketing/ads for a teacher.
5. Work through the recruitment process.
6. Appoint students to teacher and introduce.

Things to consider:

7. Do you have the necessary resources?
    a. premises, equipment etc.
8. Do you have a budget for the expenses of expansion?
    a. premises, equipment, marketing.
9. Do you have the time and energy to develop the expansion?
10. Have you considered the extra responsibilities (financial, HR and other) of expansion?
11. Have you done realistic financial projections?
12. Decided what to pay the teacher and how? Contractor or employee?
13. Do your lesson policies suit a second teacher, or need a review?
14. Will you train or mentor your teacher(s)?

The Results?

Because Lauren put the time into preparation and planning, she had a 90% uptake of lessons from those on her waiting list to her new teacher.

She was able to show them that they were still under her care, if not her weekly lessons. Students and parents were able to see her commitment and professionalism from her first communications with them as she clearly laid out the necessary steps of what would happen.

In the same way through preparation of the recruitment procedures, Lauren was confident in her chosen teacher, whose easily transition into the business was evidence that the systems and mentoring Lauren prepared prior to their start were worthwhile.

It is now roughly 18 months since Lauren took on her teacher and I am pleased to say that person is still happily working with Lauren and between them they are close to capacity again! A very pleasing situation for them all!

From a profitability viewpoint Lauren was able to increase her profit by increased student numbers (an additional 20 weekly, approximately) from which she earned 40% of the lesson fees.

ACTION STEPS

1. Decide on what level you wish to expand to next
2. Prepare
   a. Create a list of resources needed
   b. Budget for resources including marketing
3. Plan
   a. Who is responsible for each task
   b. Detail the "what " and "how" of tasks
   c. Prepare timeframes for all tasks
4. Execute the plans when they are realistic, clear and achievable.

Having successfully expanded up a level of the MSS Ladder, you may be interested in continuing further expansion.

The basic principles of expansion are the same across all levels, however the details and size of tasks will vary at each level to some degree. For example employing your first and only teacher, even though perhaps scary (whilst also exciting) will not be quite as complex as employing multiple teachers across multiple locations. Managing the recruitment process will be significantly different in time required based on the volume of responses expected but also in the complexity of requirements including scheduling that will determine your ideal recruits and perhaps balancing their skills, availability and so forth.

But what's next?

Would you consider further expansion?

For example, you may have started this journey as a "One Person Show", and have now taken on your first teacher to expand into offering instruments that you don't personally teach yourself.

So, there is the possibility of moving further up the Music School Success Ladder by expanding with more teachers and/or more locations.

Scary? Maybe… but also exciting perhaps?

Of course you might already have reached the level of expansion, or the size of the business that you are totally satisfied with. If so that is AWESOME! You are to be congratulated on knowing what suits you!

PART 3

MOVING UP THE MUSIC SCHOOL SUCCESS LADDER

CHAPTER 10

THE ROADIE

I think of myself as one of the lucky ones.

I had supportive parents who allowed and encouraged me to learn music from a young age AND to choose it as my career, no questions asked, no pressure to do anything else. This meant that I started first as a student musician through my school years but then instantly became a music teacher at the same time I entered university by starting to teach some family friends. So in reality I "skipped" the roadie level of the Music School Success Ladder.

Whether you start at Roadie level, Chorus Line or as I did a "One Person Show", you are beginning your journey on the Music School Success ladder in what is known as the FOUNDATION STAGE.

I've known lots of other "not so lucky" musicians and music teachers who for a myriad of different reasons, some being their own choice and some imposed upon them, were working in non-musical careers. Actually they desperately wanted to work in music as a career instead of what they choose or had chosen for them because it is what they were most passionate about.

When I refer to the Roadie level of the MSS Ladder, I am essentially referring to people who are musicians but who have not yet started to

teach. They may be working full or part time in non-musical jobs, OR they may even be performing musicians, just not teaching.

Regardless where a "Roadie" is working, often the biggest hurdle for them is how to get started as a Music Teacher without sacrificing whatever income or lifestyle they currently have. They lack "business" knowledge and they lack students which means they lack income from teaching.

POSITIVES/BENEFITS OF ROADIE LEVEL:

- Music can be an enjoyable "hobby"
- Music can be that thing you turn to to relieve all stresses

NEGATIVES / DISADVANTAGES OF ROADIE LEVEL:

- Not working with music at all!
- Frustration at spending so much time away from music activities!

CASE STUDY

Take Peter S for example. Peter is a fantastic guitarist who had toured with numerous bands but had reached a point where he wanted to settle down in one place with his family and provide a more stable income and life through a combination of local band gigs and regular teaching.
Peter thought his only issue was finding students until he actually found some, then he found there was a lot more to do than just teach!

He soon realised that there was a whole lot more "stuff" he needed to learn before he could be comfortable and confident in what he was doing, let alone be able to manage the admin side of what teaching entails! How was he to know about timetables, payment systems, studio policies and so on?

Peter's predicament is a common one. He has the musical skills and the musical experience to draw upon for the content of his lessons, so it's not the actual teaching that was his concern. He knew he could be an inspiring teacher in his area of expertise, rock guitar and rock bands, but how did he translate that into a viable and regular teaching income or teaching business?

ROADIE LEVEL PROBLEM – Lack of Business Knowledge

Of course Peter could have done what many of us do, and make it up as he went along, learning from trial and error, but he had a family he needed to support and didn't have time or money to waste making mistakes! He also was essentially trying to transition from creating income from tour gigs into creating income from regular teaching, so he needed it to happen sooner rather than later!

SOLUTION

Peter had great musical experience and great communication skills, so he was a naturally effective teacher. He just needed to develop the music school business know-how to be able to achieve his goals

- Read everything you can about setting up a business
- Read and re-read this book and contact me for help!
- Listen to podcasts on starting a business
- Network with other business owners
- Join online forums or social media business groups (LinkedIn and Facebook have lots)
- Find a mentor or coach

ROADIE to CHORUS LINE ACTION STEPS

1. HR – Set aside time after work or weekends to start teaching or teacher training
2. IT – Get connected and build networks
3. Ops – Do a "stocktake" of what resources you already have to start your music school (Phase 1 of MSS evolution)
4. Finance – Know your $. What income do you really need to make the switch to teaching. Work out EXACTLY what annual/quarterly/monthly/weekly income you need to generate and then "reverse engineer" that into how many hours of teaching, how many classes, how many students, how much you need to charge in fees to be able to achieve that income (Part of Phase 1 of MSS Evolution)
5. Legal – Get registered to teach
6. Merch – NA
7. Marketing – Contact local music schools, shops
8. IP – Research and decide WHAT you can/want to teach. Work out what level of the MSS Ladder is your goal – is it a one Person Show? Or do you want to employ others/open a retail studio or something else?

CHAPTER 11

THE CHORUS LINE

I have had several periods during my musical journey, where I have been "employed" by someone other than my own company.

When I first graduated from university, I continued my private teaching from home and in students homes, but I was employed as a full-time classroom teacher and instrumental co-ordinator at Santa Maria Catholic Girls College. There have been several other times when I had a hankering for classroom teaching and being part of the school environment as a staff member, hence I returned to classroom teaching as a replacement full-time secondary music teacher at Marcellin College at one time, a part-time secondary music classroom and choir director at CLC another time, and a part-time classroom, choir and band director at Viewbank Primary School at another time. All whilst continuing as Director of Wendy's Music company.

Sounds crazy right? It certainly was full-on busy, but that seems to be a consistent trend in my life! I am always looking to improve and develop what I'm doing.

There was also a time early in my career as my young family were appearing that I left full-time classroom teaching, continued teaching privately but also took up teaching a few afternoons a week as a "contracted" teacher working for another music education company,

Creative Music at one time and Mobile Music at another. This type of teaching, when you are working for someone else is what is known as being on the "Chorus Line" level of the Music School Success Ladder. Being employed as a classroom teacher however is not the typical "Chorus Line" gig. Most commonly it's when you are a vocal or instrumental teacher working for a music school which could be small or large, at a school, a retail studio or in homes.

When you are a vocal or instrumental teacher for someone else the benefits are that you usually have less responsibility for administration and can focus almost exclusively on the actual delivery of the lessons. You are still in the FOUNDATION STAGE of the MSS Ladder. In most cases the work required outside actual lesson time is very minimal, other than whatever lesson preparation you actual wish to do. Teaching for another company enables you to gain teaching experience and perhaps learn from other teachers within the company. As your experience increases lesson planning should also decrease. In the instance of larger companies, I would hope however that lesson content would be provided and potentially a method or program to follow that minimises the need for you to "work it out yourself".

In my own music School, known simply as Wendy's Music, I am in the final stages of turning my 110 music method books, resources and training into an online delivery program where teachers will have the lesson plans at their fingertips delivered to their students online with only a click or two on their keyboard. We are also changing our business model to enable teachers to be independent and earn more than a contracted or employed teacher but have the benefits of being part of a large company.

For more about this you can visit www.WendysMusic.com.au and check out the Teachers section.

My reason for choosing to teach for another company was essentially to fill a gap in my working week with as little effort as possible. I was given several hours of teaching for which I had to do very little preparation and virtually no administration, both of which suited me at the time as I also had a husband and three young children to look after. Having said that though, I must admit that I have the most incredibly supportive husband who, for our entire married life, has readily jumped in and done whatever household task, childcare, taxi driving, shopping or whatever to help keep a semblance of sanity and organisation in our busy house! The main attraction though for most teachers is that quite often when working for someone else's music school you are given an allocation of several students, or several hours of teaching in one slab, you don't necessarily have to wait for it to build up. This for me was attractive too, but I only ever had the intention of doing this work for a short period of time. Essentially I had perhaps two afternoons of work with Creative Music which I then cut down to one afternoon when my own private students increased, and then again stopped entirely as they increased further.

It's a delicate balancing act for which you need to know your numbers and also be prepared to work perhaps longer hours for a short time with the long term gains in mind.

POSITIVES /BENEFITS OF CHORUS LINE LEVEL:

- less responsibility
- few tasks required outside lesson time
- a time to build teaching experience
- instant student list handed to you.

Conversely though when you are a vocal or instrumental teacher for someone else, your income is less per student or hour than if you are working as the owner and responsible for recruiting, administration and everything to do with lessons. Your control of things such as your timetable, lesson content, materials, communication and so on is often also limited when you are an employed or contracted teacher.

Having less responsibility and little administration can be very attractive to some teachers. It may be attractive as a stepping stone to the next level of the MSS ladder where you become a sole owner-operator. Many university students are often found at this level as they gain teaching experience at a time they can't afford to spend hours on administration or learning business skills.

In the same way if you plan it well, you can simultaneously be growing your own private students whilst working for someone else. Just be VERY careful that you do not in any way breach the trust of your employer by deliberately or unwittingly "poaching" students from their business.

NEGATIVES / DISADVANTAGES OF CHORUS LINE LEVEL:

- less control of lesson content
- less control of timetable
- less control of almost everything
- lesson fees shared with business owner
- hard to find time to grow your own private student list
- difficulty balancing income from employed work whilst building private teaching

When you are teaching for someone else, regardless if it is a large or small company, it can appear a bit of a roadblock to growing your own

music teaching business. In actuality it can give you great insight into how a music school can be run – from both sides of the tracks, the teacher and the business owner.

You are in a position to observe how the business is being run, what you like and don't like about it, and therefore gain some ideas of how you would like YOUR music school to be, if and when you are ready to develop it.

You could have informal conversations with other teachers and staff working alongside you and also get their impressions to add to your observation.

You can also use this time to develop marketing ideas and even begin to use them when you are ready to start building your own student list.

1. Prepare – working out what resources you already have
2. Dream – deep thinking to unveil your deepest desires (music related!)
3. Design – planning how to turn the dreams into reality
4. Build – doing the work to bring the plans to life
5. Live – testing and tweaking time
6. Share – making an impact with your music school
7. Expand – growing in size, responsibility, income and students

There should be no reason why you can't begin to recruit students privately whilst working for another person or company BUT (as I mentioned before) please be ethical about it and do not poach students – doing so will only result in ruining your professional reputation, something not easily recovered.

CASE STUDY

Piano teacher Christine came to us as a totally inexperienced teacher but with good musical skills and a great personality for teaching children particularly. Christine has worked with us for several years, participating fully in our teacher training, using our teaching program and most importantly gaining confidence and experience teaching.

When Christine approached us for teaching work, she was unsure whether she would be considered "suitable" and whether in fact she would be able to attract any students at all. By joining a company she was able to exceed her expectations and has a full timetable of students now. As a mature person Christine also appreciates and understands the volume of work needed to find and manage students and a music school. She is happy not to have that responsibility so she can focus on her teaching. Her gratitude and enthusiasm for her lessons is refreshing!

CHORUS LINE PROBLEM – Achieving enough income

Getting your first position as a music teacher in a music school or studio feels great! However remember the old saying "Don't put all your eggs in one basket!" It can be hard to earn a decent living working only at one studio or music school when you are new to teaching, as often they won't want to trust you with too many students until you have proven yourself.

If you teach mostly children then your hours of teaching will be restricted to maybe three or four hours after school on weekdays and then whatever time you want to devote to teaching on the weekend.

When lessons are offered during the year it is also important to consider - are you only going to offer them in school terms? If so this will restrict your income by about 25%.

SOLUTION

Assess your financial needs i.e. what income you need personally after all expenses are paid. Always allow a small buffer i.e. aim to make slightly more income than your minimum requirement in case of unexpected changes.

Start by working for several music companies at the same time. A couple of days working in a school program with one company, a couple of afternoons with one music school and another few with another or something along those lines can help keep the money coming in.

It's not easy as every company has different policies, procedures or programs, but it does mean you are not reliant on only one company/ school!

You can move from being a Roadie doing non-music teaching work by adding some teaching after hours or weekends, increasing this until you can start to cut back on the non-teaching work. In the same way you can move from teaching for someone else into teaching privately as quickly or gradually as you want to make it happen.

Your priority should be to maximise any available time for private students, BUT and this is a big one, PLEASE be respectful of the people or companies for whom you are already teaching and do not under any circumstances be tempted to "poach" students you are teaching to your own private teaching. This would not only be unethical, but

ultimately shows to those parents/students, that you are not trustworthy or respectful, regardless of contracts and agreements. You should be concentrating on attracting students who want to learn specifically from YOU and who have chosen you above other organisations for whatever reason(s) you offer.

Your flexibility to teach whenever students are available is going to help your numbers grow, and as demand grows, you can get more fussy later.

Would you like income all year round? Why not offer lessons all year round? Or offer "special" classes in school holidays instead.

Alternately if you want a break in school holidays, then you'll need to earn enough during the term to counterbalance the lack of income in the school holidays – this can amount to as many as twelve weeks of the year in Australia… almost 25% of the year! So consider your options carefully!

Consider teaching adults or preschool students during the day if you can't get into schools or another option is that you can consider taking beginner groups where the pay per hour can be higher.

CHORUS LINE TO ONE PERSON SHOW ACTION STEPS:

"I need help to start teaching."

1. HR – Set aside time to start building your own school./teaching/ self-employment
2. IT - Research the technology that can support your Fin, Ops, Merch, A and M and IP
3. Ops – Plan policies and systems to administer everything – find location. Prepare, dream, design your next step.
4. Fin – Balance employed income and self-employed income. Know your financial needs so you can balance the different types of work to achieve it at all times. Knowing that position at all times allows you to know when to drop the lower paid employed work and how many private students you need to balance the changeover
5. Legal – Research required permits and registrations for your teaching location
6. Merch – Decide on program offerings and prices
7. Marketing – Plan how to get the word out.
8. IP – Research, test and document everything in admin and lesson programs. Observe and learn from every music school, teacher and business you are in contact with.

CHAPTER 12

THE ONE PERSON SHOW

There are many musicians who like me started their teaching career by teaching friends of the family.

I had just been accepted into Melbourne University Conservatorium of Music and my proud parents recruited my first few students from amongst their friends' families (without my knowing, if I recall correctly!)

I started teaching at age 17 (when I completed secondary school) with no knowledge of HOW to teach or WHAT to teach, but because I was deemed knowledgeable enough to get a place at a prestigious university I was considered ready to teach.

I have no recollection of how I decided what my fees would be, but I do remember asking my own piano teacher (who encouraged me to start teaching) what book I should get students to buy as a teaching method. She of course recommended what she had been using for YEARS, *The Leila Fletcher Piano Course*, and armed with that information off I went!

WOW, what a learning curve!

Some of the big hurdles that stand out to me from that time were:

1. How to explain musical concepts to students
2. What to do if they DIDN'T understand the first time
3. How to deal with students not practising
4. How much work to give them each week
5. How to motivate them to "finish" pieces
6. How to stop myself from expecting "perfection" from beginner students (this took me a while to learn!)

Being a One Person Show means exactly what it says – you are the only person in your music school. You are in charge of Teaching, Timetables, Payments, Communications, everything! Because you are still possibly learning how to be a teacher and how to run a business, you are still in the FOUNDATION STAGE of the MSS Ladder.

So there I was, a 17-year-old, horribly embarrassed having to ask adults, friends of my mum, to give me money! And of course as you can imagine as time went by, sometimes they would forget, and "promise" it for next time… so then it became a matter of keeping track of who paid, when and how much and having to give receipts (eventually, so I could prove to them when they needed to pay again without argument).

Of course there was also the issue of lessons being cancelled at the last minute for flimsy reasons – a forgotten clash with a birthday party, their child is feeling tired today etc etc which meant of course they didn't want to pay for the lesson even though I was already waiting for them!

When you first start teaching for yourself, you will be tempted to be really accommodating to your students, flexible with cancellations, payments and so forth, but I STRONGLY encourage you to set yourself up in a professional manner that would suit YOU if your teaching schedule was

PACKED and you had a waiting list.

Why should you accept late cancellations and not get paid for time you can't allocate to someone else?

Why should you provide the lessons and get paid AFTER they are given?

WHEN you get to the point you have a full schedule and a waiting list, you will be wanting to make use of every teaching minute possible, so YOU need to set the rules earlier in your career rather than later. Don't be tempted by the "I've got to keep them happy or they won't continue with me" thinking pattern, because some students just aren't worth keeping, they take too much energy and time, they distract you from the valuable, reliable students.

Instead of focussing on trying to keep everyone happy, keep YOURSELF happy and healthy and unstressed first, so you can provide great teaching, and that way your students will get so much value they will come back regardless of your "rules".

Despite the responsibility of being a One Person Show and the extra time to organise everything to do with your lessons, the benefit of the freedom it gives you cannot be discounted.

There is no-one to tell you when, how or what to teach, no-one to make unrealistic demands on your time. Best of all though, whatever lesson fee you decide to charge, you get to keep it all! Well, all except the amount needed to cover any costs you may have to operate your business such as membership fees, advertising, printing, travel to lessons, equipment and so on…

If however my description of what can happen scares you and you're starting to wonder if you can manage the admin and the teaching (plus of course finding students to start with!) then I have a solution for you! Having worked on both sides of the "fence", I know what it is like to be a lowly paid subcontractor and employee, but also I know how time consuming and expensive it is to manage a studio, school program, teachers and students.

Here's the solution:

A full service that

1. Finds students for you
2. Provides all the timetable software complete with reminders to students
3. Does online payment for you
4. Gives teacher training as needed
5. Provides teaching resources and programs as needed.

Become a member and remain an independent teacher and chose how and what you teach but get paid a VERY high percentage of the lesson fees.

Learn more on my website: www.WendysMusic.com.au/music-teacher-membership/

POSITIVES/BENEFITS OF ONE PERSON SHOW

- FREEDOM!
- Choose when and how much you work
- Choose how and what you teach
- Get paid the full student lesson fee

NEGATIVES / DISADVANTAGES OF ONE PERSON SHOW

- RESPONSIBILITY!
- Getting paid only happens if YOU organise the payment, which may mean chasing people!
- You don't have colleagues to learn from
- You have no "back-up" person if you get sick, or can't teach for some reason
- You are required to do all administration
- You are responsible for finding students
- You are responsible for keeping students happy!
- You pay the cost of setting up a studio and its resources

CASE STUDY

Dimitrios is a good example of someone who moved from being on "the Chorus Line" to being a "One Person Show". Dimitrios started teaching several afternoons a week at one of our studios for several years and then began to teach his own students privately until he had sufficient to cut down the hours he taught with us. Progressively he taught less with us and built his own private teaching more until he became fully independent.

You might think from an employer's perspective that it is disappointing to spend time and money training teachers only to have them leave and build their own teaching practice, and it is in part disappointing, however you have to see both sides. Dimitrios was a reliable and good teacher for our company for several years, you must consider that to be worthwhile. From a higher perspective, I feel very positive about the help I have given hundreds of teachers to get started on their teaching. Those who were interested and willing to learn, were able to fast-track their teaching skills and I was happy to help. The alternative is to leave

inexperienced teachers to trial and error and make unnecessary mistakes which ultimately impacts on students they are supposed to be inspiring and guiding. I'd prefer to provide students with the best quality teaching we can provide than be concerned that I am wasting my time with a teacher who will ultimately leave our company.

ONE PERSON SHOW LEVEL PROBLEM – Unreliable income

At this level, as I mentioned earlier, it is your choice to try and be everyone's "best friend" and allow them to cancel or change lessons at the last minute, take weeks off mid-term, withdraw at a moment's notice and so on – all in the hope that they will stick with you because you are so flexible! Doing this is not sustainable or professional and only leads to you being taken advantage of and basically not respected for what you are worth!

The result is that your income from lessons is also very unreliable, you never know for sure how many lessons you will be giving from one week to the next, so your income will change also from one week to the next!

SOLUTION:

Carefully consider what your income needs to be then set guidelines to ensure that students value their time with you. Make-up policies, withdrawal policies and so forth are essential to a professional music teacher.

Recently I heard a teacher say that she couldn't afford to fill up her after-school times as she then couldn't fit in all the necessary make-up lessons needed at the end of each term. How unfortunate it is, that music

teachers are expected to change lessons around and make themselves available at unsocial hours for make up lessons, or disrupt their own holidays simply for the convenience of the student. For those teachers who stipulate "no make-ups" or put a limit of when a make-up will be given (same week/term/30 days), the importance of attending the regular lesson time increases significantly and the teacher's timetable stabilises as a result. No need to factor in spaces for make ups that gain you no extra income!

Frequency of payments can also be a contributing factor to unreliable income. Accepting weekly cash payments may have some attraction when you start, but the hassle of asking for it each week, recording it each week, and the possibility a lesson will be cancelled at late notice and then no payment at all? Not worth it.

Monthly or term or semester payments mean your student commits for that period at least. You have the money upfront (hopefully) and therefore some security of income for that time.

As mentioned previously you can choose to offer regular lessons, holiday programs, workshops or such during school holidays to help make your income more regular when regular lessons are often put on hold. These holiday activities might even bring new students.

ONE PERSON SHOW TO LEADING PERSON ACTION STEPS:

1. HR – Set up a teacher recruitment system
2. IT – Refine and test the technology to support your Fin, Ops, Merch, M and IP systems as they grow
3. Ops – Adapt policies to include staff, find and set up locations with equipment and resources
4. Finance – Balance profit derived from your teaching with profit to achieve your desired income. Set up budgets for business activities. Add payroll facility
5. Legal – Get advice re changing your business structure as you take on employees. Review leases
6. Merchandise – Review your program offerings with more teachers. Consider instrument, equipment, book sales
7. Marketing – How will you recruit more students for more teachers? Signage, website etc
8. IP – Document your programs and set up training for them

CHAPTER 13

THE LEADING PERSON

What is it that makes us want to go beyond teaching for ourselves, to teaching for ourselves with the addition of other teachers for whom we need to be responsible? What makes us want to enter the ENTERPRISE STAGE?

In most cases it's about increasing our income and often the idea starts because we have a full timetable ourselves and are unable to take on more students. Perhaps there is a waiting list of students that you don't want to lose.

Sometimes the expansion is instigated by a different opportunity. Perhaps you have a friend who wants to start teaching and you see an opportunity that will work for you both. Perhaps you have students whose siblings want to learn an instrument you do not teach and you see an opportunity to add another instrument and gain students through this variety of classes.

In my case, I was a young mother of 26, teaching six days a week, around 30 hours teaching with a constant waiting list of students for my piano and theory lessons. I wanted to capitalise on the reputation I had developed (including the waiting list) and decrease my own teaching hours without decreasing my income. So my husband agreed to set up an additional teaching room with a separate access and start on

the interesting journey of expanding my music school to include other teachers.

So having decided to jump into this expansion, a whole heap of questions arose:

- Where do I find a piano teacher who wants to work for me?
- Why would they want to work for me rather than do it themselves?
- What are the characteristics of the teacher I need?
- How much do I pay them?
- How often do I pay them?
- What resources do I need to supply?
- Do I need to train them?
- What are my legal obligations?
- Do I need "for real" contracts?
- Do I have to deal with their tax or superannuation?
- How do I manage their timetable, or do they?
- How much responsibility will I give them over organisation?
- How much responsibility will I give them over lesson content?
- Do I want to be responsible their curriculum?

As you can see, there were many questions, some of which I had BEFORE I started the process of finding teachers, and some that I only realised along the way.

I remember quite vividly the first dilemma of what sort of teacher I wanted.

I had planned the day, the hours, those logistical things, but when it came to selecting my first teacher it was actually very difficult!

Firstly, what do I need to put into an advertisement for a piano teacher?

In those days you placed an ad in your local paper (and possibly the city paper) and run it for several weeks whilst waiting impatiently for results.

Next I needed to be able to make a selection from the resumes received, some of which read really well and others I just knew wouldn't be suitable as they didn't fit my logistic or qualifications requirements – this is why writing a clear ad featuring the most important requirements is important! First lesson learned!

Once my shortlist was chosen, then came the interview dilemma:

What questions do I ask in an interview?
How do I judge or compare their responses when they are so different?
How do I balance the pros and cons of each candidate when no-one is a "perfect fit"?

I remember spending hours and days deliberating over who to choose and then when I finally picked up the phone and offered it to them – they were no longer available! Of course they had applied to other places! I had taken too long to decide and they of course needed to accept work where it was offered, so I missed out!

Deciding on what were the most important characteristics in a teacher became a priority fairly early in my expansion. Personality, communication skills, philosophy, flexibility and the ability to work as part of a team, became more important than extensive experience and highest qualification.

Finally I found my first teacher and another learning curve began!

Despite spending what I considered to be significant time talking through details of how things would work, what my expectations were and so forth, I soon learned that staff needed to be given VERY specific not just verbal, but written, instructions if I wanted them to remember or comply with particular ways of doing things. Teachers who are working for you for a small number of hours per week are more than likely also working for someone else, including themselves, so their priorities are somewhat different to yours, and their memory of verbal instructions not always as good as yours!

Learning what "training" teachers required has taken years of trial and error. I've written teaching manuals, procedure manuals, recorded training videos, run live workshops, observed and critiqued lessons and in the last few years have put together an online training that continues to evolve and improve as technology develops. Ultimately it is the outcomes of training that need to be considered for it to be effective.

POSITIVES/BENEFITS OF LEADING PERSON LEVEL:

- Increase income by taking more students than you can personally handle
- Expand by offering other instruments
- Have colleagues to work with
- Can expand slowly if desired using home studio or small studio
- Gives you the control over lessons, and admin to whatever degree you wish
- Enables the possibility of decreased teaching load to offset additional admin

NEGATIVES / DISADVANTAGES OF LEADING PERSON LEVEL:

- Adds legal and financial responsibilities for staff
- Additional administration with increased students
- Additional systems and documentation for student and staff
- Variations in teaching style, content and outcomes
- Risk of reputation loss if staff not well managed and trained
- Risk of teachers being unreliable

CASE STUDY

Kristin came to me for help when her studio was overflowing with students and she saw a great opportunity to build upon a solid reputation that she had built over many years. She had established a curriculum that she liked and produced good results and she had systems and procedures in place that worked for her to run her studio smoothly, but she was really concerned about how to go about recruiting the "right" teacher for her studio.

Essentially within one session we were able to determine the two main components that she need to put considered thought into:

1. The Logistics
2. The Characteristics

The Logistics include things like:

- What days and times they are required?
- How many hours/days are they required?
- School terms only or not?
- Where will they teach?
- Flexibility
- What equipment do they need to be able to provide (own keyboards, computer etc)?

The Characteristics include things like:

- Age or maturity
- Experience
- Qualifications
- Teaching method
- Teaching philosophy
- Personality

ONE PERSON SHOW LEVEL PROBLEM – Finding students

One of the most common problems I hear about from teachers at this level are that they don't know how to find students.

It's different finding students when you first start, to when you are established and different again when you are finding students for other teachers.

You may start out teaching friends and family, then get some referrals or siblings starting, but when you have the responsibility of filling time for another teacher, it may not be enough to compensate for the natural attrition of students starting to learn and then chasing for basketball or ballet instead.

Often there is no problem finding students for your first teacher as you have may developed a waiting list from your own personal teaching. If not, or if the numbers do not naturally continue to remain steady or grow, then finding students for another teacher is a little different to finding students for yourself, even if they are working for and with you.

When you are the only teacher, you can confidently answer questions about lesson content, outcomes and other details, but it can be more difficult answering those questions on behalf of your teaching staff.

Sometimes convincing siblings or friends of my current students to learn from my "staff" teacher was difficult as they have an expectation that they must have the "leading" teacher, or the one they are used to!

SOLUTION:

Finding students when you are starting out is tough as no-one knows you exist as a teacher. My first suggestion is to get yourself listed on every relevant music teacher directory or similar websites.

Some directories are free to list , however you will be often one of hundreds of teachers competing for students, so you will need to write an impressive profile to stand out.

Alternately you can become a member of a service that provides students, admin, training, resources and support here www.WendysMusic.com.au/music-teacher-membership/

Secondly, you need to show students why they should come to your music school. The most common reason music teachers don't know how to find students is that they don't make themselves or their music school stand out!

Do you "just offer piano lessons?" Or do you offer "piano lessons that achieve X, Y or Z?" There is competition almost everywhere, at least that's what teachers say who also complain they can't find students.

So if this is you, then you need to sit down and figure out what it is that you can offer that is "different" to all your competition, and articulate this in every piece of advertising or marketing that you are doing.

Oh yes – you also have to do some of that – advertising and marketing – students don't just "happen" along, you usually have to make yourself known to enough people first before the referrals kick in!

Third, make sure you know how to "sell" your school or your teacher(s) to potential students. Know what they are good at, what personality traits, skills, experience students would value. Promote all the services you offer to the potential student whilst also finding out what they want.

LEADING PERSON TO PRINCIPAL ACTION STEPS:

"I enjoy teaching and creating my own school."

1. HR – Review systems and supervision of staff in multiple locations
2. IT – Review hardware and software systems for multiple locations and staff
3. Ops – Review management of schedules, set up more locations
4. Financial – Set up financial tracking systems for multi locations
5. Legal – Get advice on leasing multiple premises
6. Merch – Consolidate programs across all locations
7. M – Expand systems for multiple locations
8. IP – Update all documentation

CHAPTER 14

THE PRINCIPAL

It was a couple of years after my third child was born that my music school went to another level.

I had continued to teach privately five or six days a week whilst all three of my children were growing up – one of the perks of being a home based music teacher in fact! I was however finding the afternoon and evening teaching to be rather like a juggling match as I now had one child at school, one in kinder and a toddler (and my incredibly supportive husband still doing amazing things!) If I recall correctly, the change started because I had a school aged child and was teaching a number of students from her school. I was also one of those parents who "got involved" in school activities such as helping with reading, excursions and so on to support my shy eldest child settle into school. I had become familiar with the teacher at the school who ran their limited music program and was able to negotiate to start teaching students that I had been taking at home, at school during school hours instead! Benefits to parents of convenience, to the school (they could now say they had an instrumental music program) and benefit to me being that my after-school load was decreased.

Having negotiated my first school successfully, I then set about doing the same at several other local primary schools from where I had several students learning piano also. This built up to six primary schools in a

very short space of time which I taught across five weekdays. Of course with such convenience, the student list at each school grew once I started newsletter notices broadcasting what I was doing (in addition to the usual referrals) to the degree that once again I faced the dilemma of having more teaching than I could manage. As part of this process I deliberately started offering lessons in multiple instruments (given I had studied many myself) and by getting each school and instrument started, I was then able to progressively hand off an instrument or school to a "staff " teacher – on my team of growing teachers.

This meant my income would keep growing and allow me to decrease my own teaching hours to a minimum amount of a couple of days' worth at home whilst "my" teachers, took all the school lessons for me and for which I did the administration. At this level I was still part of the ENTERPRISE STAGE of the MSS ladder.

As with every level of expansion though, I discovered many difficulties. The biggest difficulty as your school grows is the management of staff. The more staff you have, the more opportunity for choosing an unsatisfactory teacher, for inconsistency in lesson delivery, for admin error and increased issues of teacher turnover. PLUS the logistics of having the right teacher available on the day a school has a room available and so forth, are certainly interesting components!

POSITIVES /BENEFITS OF PRINCIPAL LEVEL:

- Balance between own private teaching and administration can be achieved
- Building a team of teachers to potentially broaden classes offered
- Building a team of teachers to enable greater flexibility of timetabling
- Increased teaching income
- Less dependence upon one or two teachers
- Increased potential for merchandising income

NEGATIVES /DISADVANTAGES OF PRINCIPAL LEVEL:

- Increased responsibility of payroll and other financial and legal obligations
- More administration required as student and staff numbers grow
- Increased risk of teachers "doing their own thing"
- Increased risk of teachers leaving - teacher "turnover"

CASE STUDY

I had known Cath for a long time when she contacted me for help about her music school. She had over 200 students and was teaching herself in around three or four schools taking keyboard groups, but also employing teachers to take violin, guitar and woodwind lessons in six schools local to her area.

Cath's problems were centred around the administration and operations of her business, and her Human Resources area (or HR) which is anything to do with staff.

You would expect that the more students and teachers you have in your business, the more administration you need to do – simple! However when teaching in a school environment particularly when you are considered an "itinerant" or independent teacher, not employed in any way by the school itself, the admin is substantially increased.

Not only do you need to keep good communication with parents, students and teachers, but now there is another layer of communication needed with the school admin staff and perhaps coordinator. You also need to work in with the timetable and systems the school has in place. So it was no surprise to me when Cath described her frustration of spending hours

and hours simply trying to keep the basic operations of her business working.

Cath had been running her business also for many years and was a highly experienced teacher, but she needed someone to look at the bigger picture and see what could be improved, someone who wasn't stuck in the daily grind. Her website was already very informative, but she wasn't utilising it fully for her administration. Her school programs were running well and she had built solid relationships with each school and the principal at each school, but she was concerned that a change of principal at one school could mean losing that program. There were also some issues with her teaching staff that concerned her.

After a thorough review of what she had in place and where she felt there were problems, we were able to make several significant improvements and a number of smaller improvements including that she:

1. Update her payment system to become more automated through her website
2. Start using an email auto responder to automate a certain amount of email communication
3. Set up teacher contracts that covered all the points of concern
4. Set up school contracts and a system of renewing them

These were four fairly major changes which took a little time to put into effect and did involve some research before all were finalised and in place. All were effective in helping Cath improve her situation, relieve her concerns and give her back some significant time from manual payments and communications.

PRINCIPAL LEVEL PROBLEM – Finding suitable teachers

As I've described above, many teachers struggle with the responsibility of taking on their first "staff" teacher, regardless of whether they are an "employee" or an independent "contractor".

There are so many aspects that need to be considered and decided upon before anyone starts otherwise you may find that they end up "running the show" with their demands, ideas, expectations taking priority over yours.

It may sound like an easy task to find a teacher when you have a waiting list of students for them, but there are so many ways it can also be very difficult.

Firstly, I urge you to refrain from just asking friends and family to join your teaching team, unless you are really confident in their teaching ability, communication skills and know you will be able to work with them on a professional level.

What constitutes a "suitable" teacher?

It's not just about having the right instrumental or musical skills.

You might want someone super-creative, able to develop new programs or conversely you might need someone willing to follow a set program. There are lots of logistics that need to work, most importantly availability needs to match and location needs to be a sustainable distance.

Do you need someone with formal qualifications? Or is years of performing experience suitable? What musical styles do they need experience in? Do they need experience preparing students for exams and so on.

SOLUTION

Start by brainstorming about all the desired skills you require in a teacher.

Now consider the logistics of exactly when, where, how, etc they are required.

Decide what sort of personality and qualifications you require.

Make a list of as many questions as possible designed to find out whether each applicant fits the profile you have now built.

Develop a list and then a manual of procedures, resources and references for your "staff".

Research contracts and payment options.

Also make a list of what you can provide FOR the approved teacher – what's in it for them? Pay, increased hours, training and support. They need to WANT the position and want to KEEP the position, so it has to be attractive for them, not just for you!

Construct a simple ad that you can place on social media, employment sites etc, but make sure it spells out the basics so you don't get swamped with inappropriate applicants.

PRINCIPAL TO MANAGER ACTION STEPS:

"I am creating my Music School team."

1. HR – Managing your time
2. IT – Make it work for you
3. Ops – Keep it efficient
4. Fin – Manage the money
5. Leg – Review your personal and business tax structure
6. Merch – Review sales funnels
7. A and M – Build a brand
8. IP – Document YOUR admin role

CHAPTER 15

THE MANAGER

I considered myself to be at "Manager" level on the MSS ladder when I had four retail studios running in Fitzroy, Reservoir, Diamond Creek and Rosanna. We had hundreds of students, around 20 teachers of brass, woodwind, guitar, violin, drums, singing and piano. We were also running some workshop programs such as "The Little Musos" program for Preschoolers, and Holiday Programs.

At this time I wasn't teaching what I would consider regularly, although I had a small number of students and occasionally filled in when a teacher was away unexpectedly (I really can't keep out of it!) I also had several admin staff to assist with some of the studio organisation and operations, but ultimately I was the manager of all the studios — I made the decisions about marketing, programs, staff, merchandise and so on.

When operating a business with multiple locations and staff you quickly find out that systemisation in everything is important.

You need to have systems for things like:

- Enrolment procedures
- Payment procedures
- Timetable procedures
- Managing lesson policies
- Payroll procedures

- Teacher recruitment and training
- Ordering, supply and payment of books and materials for students
- Performance organisation
- Exam organisation
- Teacher, student/parent, school communications
- Marketing and advertising
- Merchandise orders and supply
- Managing teachers and so on and so forth — you get the picture!

However even with the best systemisation and thorough organisation, your music school business may not produce great results unless the quality of lessons is attracting and retaining students.

The more teaching staff you have in your music school, the more frequently you are likely to have teachers changing. It is quite natural for employed or contracted teachers to only stay in a teaching position for a few years because, as we learnt earlier, it is a natural progression for many to start teaching for themselves, or perhaps if they are a university or college student, to move into full-time school employment upon graduation.

Managing Teacher Changes

Managing teacher changes should be done with great care. Although students are familiar with having different teachers in their regular schooling — sometimes a different teacher for each subject, or even a shared classroom or pastoral teacher — but when it comes to private music lessons, the expectation is often quite different. When having an individual weekly session with a student, the relationship over time can becomes closer, I wouldn't encourage anyone to deliberately make "close" friends with their child students, but you do get to know a bit about their likes and dislikes and what's happening in their lives,

particularly as we often end up needing to use a bit of psychology to find triggers to motivate and encourage our students if they are having a bad day or a rough time in general. Sometimes music lessons are a genuine "outlet" for shy or "nerdy" students and they therefore put great value on the relationship they have with their teacher.

Every human is different, so personalities will vary from teacher to teacher and therefore the relationship as described can never be replicated when a teacher changes. What can make the biggest difference between a smooth transition and a distressing one, is keeping everything else to do with the lesson consistent from teacher to teacher.

For example I found out very early when employing teachers, the following points to consider and remind new teachers whilst the relationship settles and you get to know the strengths and weaknesses musically of the student:

- Keep the lesson routine the same (i.e. the activities and order of activities)
- Take careful note of how much homework was being given and maintain similarly
- NEVER criticise the previous teacher in any way
- Avoid making immediate big changes
- Aim to use the same terminology as the previous teacher, don't presume the student understands your terminology, ask them if they know these terms or those
- Have discussions with your students about choices, or plans as much as possible, include them in the decisions about music, homework etc
- Without going overboard, help the student get to know you by telling them a little about your musical journey or experience as it relates to the lesson activity

- Avoid a quick change of music or music books until value has been given and the student agrees to change

It can be quite distressing for a young student getting used to a change of teacher who has a different personality, a different way of explaining things or uses unfamiliar terminology and also a change of material to work on all happening at once. Many times I have seen that this caused young students who previously thrived in lessons to lose interest (having lost confidence) and withdraw from learning music.

Gradually over time if treated with care, the student will relax and enjoy a new person, a new perspective on learning at which point changes to lesson content and delivery can be slowly introduced. The length of time this will take, will vary with each student.

POSITIVES/BENEFITS OF MANAGER LEVEL:

- Full-time managing and developing the business
- Potential for administration assistance
- Growing team of teachers
- Potential for more locations
- Potential for more programs to be developed
- Potential for increased merchandise sales
- Less customer contact

NEGATIVES/DISADVANTAGES OF MANAGER LEVEL:

- Increased financial responsibilities
- Increased legal responsibilities
- Increased risk of inconsistent lesson quality
- Increased risk of teacher unreliability or turnover
- Increased risk of losing customer engagement
- Increased risk of losing teacher connection and loyalty

CASE STUDY

I recently met Jonathan as a fellow music school owner visiting my home town of Melbourne from his home town of Sydney. Jonathan's journey as a music school owner is a slightly unusual one, given he came from a totally different industry and was not a musician at all when he bought the business. His daughter had learnt at the school and he was looking for a local opportunity where he could use his business skills and have some fun with his family. His daughter is also now a teacher at his music school.

Learn 2 Play Music has a retail shop, private lessons in multiple instruments and also runs rock band programs and concerts for their students. Jonathan has part-time retail assistants, and a variety of instrumental teaching staff servicing his several hundred students.

When we first met, Jonathan was going through the usual task of updating his administration software to make his timetabling and payment systems less manual and more efficient. He was also on a mission to improve his student engagement and retention to therefore keep his student numbers increasing, not just maintaining them.

Young students are so used to using technology, getting instant gratification and being acknowledged for every little achievement. Learning a musical instrument takes years to "master" to even an intermediate degree of proficiency, and as professional musicians and music teachers, we have the ability to make it easy or hard for students in the way we support their early years of development.

Jonathan was exploring using technology to "game-ify" lessons. Students would log into a software platform and earn online rewards for each

login, amount of practice, goals and so forth. I will be very interested to hear how successful it has been for his music school.

PROBLEM OF MANAGER LEVEL – Student retention

Most music teachers and music schools have almost an expectation that students will automatically have the same love of learning and making music as we do. Often they start with a very minor interest, or sometimes it actually comes from the parents, so how we manage lessons and their learning can be the thing that keeps them going or quickly shows them it's not for them.

Sometimes we are so close to the music, we have such a passion, we have forgotten how hard it can be to get started or to get past a plateau.

We can make it hard by:

- Insisting on perfection for every piece of music
- Insisting on precise and perfect techniques in every aspect of playing
- Not considering the preferences of individual students
- Not having a clear path or program where students can see their progress
- Making everything too theoretical with not enough playing of music
- Introducing concepts that are irrelevant to the student's current level and interest and so on

I'm sure you get the picture!

Many of us teach as we were taught, simply because we have not been taught how to teach or what choices there are. Sometimes we limit the way we teach simply because we don't want to leave our comfort zone

and have to learn new skills. For example I was trained as a classical pianist and my first experience of improvising was at university when I was simply told "improvise for three minutes". No instruction, no guidelines, just an expectation that as an accomplished pianist, I had this skill. It was a confidence destroying experience and not one I want any of my students to encounter, so I have had to learn not only how to improvise (still not my favourite thing) and how to teach it to beginners so they are not scared to give it a try.

SOLUTION

In regards to student retention then, these would be my guidelines:

- Have a program that shows clear progress through levels
- Reward achievements along the way with prizes, points, recognition
- Enable some individualisation of the standard program
- Make lessons practical
- Have clear goals for weekly lessons, for the term, for the year etc
- Motivate with performance opportunities
- Engage with a mix of musical style including contemporary music
- Offer ensemble or band opportunities
- Plan competitions or display an achievement board.

Above all each lesson should be FUN, leaving the student with a sense of achievement, new goals, a clear path and feeling supported by their teacher.

Another important feature of retaining students, is retaining teachers and staff.

Make sure you have great recruitment systems, not just for finding new people, but for regular appraisals and feedback so they feel valued and

want to stick around.

Be sure to reward your great staff in every way you can – they need to know that YOU know what a great job they are doing.

Lastly provide extraordinary service, so your students won't even think about going elsewhere but instead will be referring friends and family to you!

MANAGER TO DIRECTOR ACTION STEPS:

> *"I have multiple teams and projects."*

1. HR – Learn to delegate and build a manager's recruitment system
2. IT – Add another manager step of user access
3. Ops – Review for manager access
4. Fin – Review systems for manager access
5. Leg – Maintain and review systems
6. Merch – Review for manager access or consider outsourcing
7. A and M – Review for manager access
8. IP – Review security for all user steps

CHAPTER 16

THE DIRECTOR

As I write this book, I could be considered to be at this "Director's" level of the MSS Ladder. Throughout my career I have moved up and down the ladder as my business model has changed. The last few years I have been doing a major review of my teaching program in addition to transitioning my business model away from retail studios and all the responsibility they entail, towards an online model.

I resumed teaching a variety of students of all ages and levels in order to test different strategies and resources that I had been developing.

The new model allows teachers to be fully independent yet provides them with admin tools and teaching content to prevent a lot of the issues I have had to overcome and that I know a lot of my coaching clients have also experienced.

You can see the membership model here www.WendysMusic.com.au/music-teacher-membership/

Being at "Director" level essentially means spending your working time managing the business and other teachers across multiple locations. Over my journey however, I have continued to do small amounts of teaching either for a few months or as an ongoing thing with a select

group of students – it seems I can't keep away from it! So I am not always the typical example!

So currently I'm teaching some piano students, but also managing over 30 teachers of piano, guitar, drums, violin, singing, flute and saxophone. Along the way I also manage to continue coaching other music teachers, developing other ventures such as this book, an online Perform Competition, writing more online coaching courses and launching the MUSIC MISSION initiative. So in some ways the only thing that indicates I am at Director level is the fact that I am teaching, all the "other" initiatives indicate I am actually at Virtuoso level waiting patiently to become an Icon! (perhaps)

When I first achieved the "Director" level I had multiple primary school programs operating in Melbourne suburbs with teachers in place at each. I then purchased another school music education company then known as "Mobile Music" which operated around twelve school programs using mobile keyboard laboratories housed in large 30-foot caravans. I also later purchased "Bellbird Music" with around six school programs.

Purchasing your competitors is a quick way to expand, but it has a lot of challenges, mostly to do with managing two systems in every aspect of your business. Two administration systems, timetabling systems, two of basically everything!

Deciding whether to purchase another business as a means of quick expansion should be based upon several things such as:

- Will you continue operating the purchased business as it has been run by the previous owner or will you expect to merge it into your current business?
- How similar is it to your current business?
- What will you need to change to merge the businesses?

- What time commitment will the new business add to your workload?
- Do you need new staff to run the new business?
- Do you need additional resources for the new business?
- Will you change the name of the purchased business to keep its history? (The previous owner may wish to keep their business name anyway)
- Will you need new signage?
- What "other" costs might there be to set it up?
- What percentage of the current business is likely to remain?

When I purchased Mobile Music and Bellbird Music, the two school-based companies, their operation was similar enough that I was able to gradually change over the fees, the payment systems, policies etc to match our original company programs.

Because my company was already offering school-based programs, it was also easy to absorb these schools into our company without having to retain the business names of the purchased companies.

Communicating to all involved parties took significant time – parents, students, schools and teachers. Some teachers from the previous company stayed with the school program that they were familiar with, but had to sign new contracts with our company first. Others left and we replaced them with teachers we already had in our system and wanted more work, or recruited new teachers. In almost every case the teachers who continued from the purchased company were the most difficult to handle as they had to get used to our systems, whereas current or new teachers took it all in their stride as being the normal way of doing things.

We did however have to introduce progressively our teaching program as it was considerably different to what had been offered by the previous owners.

When I purchased the retail music school in Rosanna known as the "Music Firm", it was a different story. At the time we purchased this music school, we had our own retail music school in the area, but I wasn't particularly thrilled with the layout of the premises, as we had issues with sound control and lack of rooms, but it was in a great location. The Music Firm however had a purpose-built building with more studio teaching rooms and a dedicated retail and office space also.

I decided that it would be worthwhile merging the two studios into one location as soon as we took over the business, however we had a very short time frame to do so. To cut a long story short, students from the Music Firm were very reluctant to learn from a new teacher with a new company, even though the location and lesson times were the same. A large part of the problem was that the previous owners had given their teachers access to all the student contact details and had in fact opened the door for those teachers to "poach" the students from the business making it extra hard to convince those students to give us a try when their previous teacher was offering to continue teaching them, even if the location was not as convenient.

There is always the issue also of doing your best to communicate changes to people by email, by letter and even by phone or text, only to find that they either don't read what you have sent them, don't take time to understand and clarify and often don't respond at all. We had this happen with several students because we had only a couple of weeks to make the transition and the result was in one or two cases unpleasant, when they arrived at the studio to find everything had changed.

POSITIVES /BENEFITS OF DIRECTOR LEVEL:

- Focus more on developing and growing your business
- No longer getting paid by the hour as a teacher
- Building a bigger team of teachers
- Ability to offer more programs
- Manager assistance
- Multiple locations and flexibility
- Increased merchandising opportunities
- Less direct customer contact
- Less direct teacher contact

NEGATIVES /DISADVANTAGES OF DIRECTOR LEVEL:

- Increased responsibility
- Increased risk of inconsistent teaching quality
- Increased risk of teacher unreliability or turnover
- More people and tasks to manage
- Increased risk of losing customer engagement
- Increased risk of losing teacher connection and loyalty

CASE STUDY

MusiqHub in New Zealand currently operates in around 196 locations around the country with a mix of independent contract teachers and franchisees. They run school programs, numerous concerts, a variety of instruments and band programs and operate a music store.

It all began with one guitar teacher, Dean in 1997, working as a One Man Show, developing his own teaching program and ultimately in 2006 connecting with other guitar teachers and using four locations as a means to expand. Dean also developed connections with music stores. Rock star concert experiences were part of the early attraction for students, and many primary schools joined.

Expansion through franchising was utilised in 2006 where teachers are resourced, trained in the program and material. The company continued to develop its offering by also expanding the instruments and band programs by connections with other groups such as School of Rock and Kids Music Company.

DIRECTOR LEVEL PROBLEM – Student poaching

What is "poaching"? It's when you find a student, assign them to a teacher within your business and at some point the student leaves your business and ends up continuing lessons privately with the same teacher. Most likely the teacher is getting paid a higher amount for what is usually the same lesson they would get within your business. Sometimes the "poaching" is therefore initiated by the teacher for that reason as they are trying to move up the MSS Ladder themselves, however sometimes it is initiated by the student/parent who thinks they may get the lessons cheaper by going direct.

How will you ever be certain that a teacher will not "poach" students from your school for their own private teaching? You can't be 100% certain, but you can make it less likely. Regular communication, opportunities and treating them as VIPs might be part of this process.

SOLUTION

Firstly, it's about the quality of the teacher. When you recruited them did you do sufficient background checks? Call referees? Did you feel they were honest and trustworthy?

Secondly you can have a written contract or agreement with the teacher that clarifies the "ownership" of the student and restrictions (which must be reasonable) upon teachers about taking over that student "ownership".

Thirdly, you should do your best to look after your teachers the best you can. This means not just how much they get paid, but the culture of the business, the leadership and support you offer.

Fourthly, if your business is able to provide more services and programs than a "One Person Show" teacher, promoting and maintaining those things with every student can help prevent them considering changing anyway!

DIRECTOR TO VIRTUOSO ACTION STEPS:

"I am a knowledgeable team leader."

1. HR – Set up systems to review regularly with managers and look for opportunities to grow
2. IT – Maintain
3. Ops – Set up systems to review regularly with managers
4. Fin – Set up systems to review regularly with managers and look for opportunities to grow
5. Leg – Maintain
6. Merch – Set up systems to review regularly with managers and look for opportunities to grow
7. A and M – Set up systems to review regularly with managers and look for opportunities to grow
8. IP – Review for current trends

CHAPTER 17

THE VIRTUOSO

Do you aspire to having a multi-location studio with staff who manage all the daily tasks and leave you to choose your daily activities and focus on the "fun" stuff, or better still a relaxed lifestyle where you are only occasionally required to work at all?

How can this be achieved?

All around the world, there are now franchise systems in almost every industry. From hamburgers, cleaning, handymen, mowing, tuition, car detailing and more. A franchise system offers a proven set of business systems, marketing systems, operational systems to operate a business which offers a UNIQUE product or service. In addition the franchisor offers ongoing support and continued development of the product or service in return for a percentage of the income or profit.

People who purchase a franchise (known as franchisees) are essentially like managers who are so committed to the success and growth of the business that they are prepared to put down their own money and join your team, in return for a higher potential yield on their investment than they would get as an employee.

At Director level, I discussed expansion through purchasing an established business, but no matter how you have grown your business,

you ultimately need great people to help you manage, maintain and possibly continue to grow that business.

The larger your organisation grows, the more demanding the responsibilities of managing the staff. You need people who can competently manage the daily operations, the marketing, merchandising and consultants to assist you oversee finance, legal and IT. Your role progressively has to become less to do with the day to day tasks of enrolments, payments, timetables and so on, and more to do with systems and procedures to maintain and grow the business.

Franchising is a well-respected way of achieving this.

One of the significant benefits of franchising your business is that the franchisee becomes not only a loyal supporter of the business but they actively maintain and grow their part of the business. A "greenfield" franchisee would start a music school from nothing, but use your systems and branding to establish more quickly than if they tried to set up alone. This means that they will be actively growing the business at their location with support from you, but much, much less support and supervision than an employed manager would need.

Hence growing your business through selling franchises can be a quicker means of growth than if your company had to do it alone. It also means that the franchisees fund the expansion for you.

One of the disadvantages of franchising compared to company owned locations is that the ongoing percentage of income will be significantly less for the franchisor than if they owned the music schools and managed them all via the company. There is however a balance with franchisees paying an upfront purchase amount before they start to enable you to

supply them with the necessary training, support and resources. So if you do your sums carefully and get advice from a good franchise lawyer or broker, your cash flow although different to running your own music school, can still be substantial. It is important however to remember that the more responsibility given to a franchisee over a manager equals more income; less responsibility equals less income as it is important that the franchisee earns enough to make it worthwhile putting in more effort than an employee.

Consider Expanding Through Franchising

However before you rush into planning to open your franchise, you should consider the following :

- Do you have a unique program or service?
- Do you have every part of your business documented?
- Is every part of your business systemised ?
- Could someone else run your business using your systems?
- Do you have a training program?
- Can you afford the legal costs involved in setting up franchise documentation?
- Are you willing to "share" your business with others?

One of the most important features that sets a franchise apart from any other business is that it offers something unique – a program, a method, a service or products that are only available through that particular company. This can be achieved by a company which owns multiple stores or in our case music schools of course, but the big difference is the scaleability. For any company to own and operate hundreds of their own stores or schools would be an incredible financial investment and in many cases would take decades to achieve (if at all). By franchising a business, not only are the people who manage each franchise more

committed because they have put their own money into the business and therefore have a vested interest in its success, but they are committed longer term.

To franchise a business though takes considerable time and preparation as everything needs to be documented, consistent branding and marketing developed and training programs devised, systems bedded down so that almost anyone could operate it AND (and this is the important one) so that they are all operated exactly the same way!

There is also the consideration of the legal documentation required. This will also take considerable time to individualise to your business and will cost thousands of dollars to set up, with annual updates needed to disclosure documents also.

However you may be determined that this is the path for you, because you have developed a program that is totally unique to you and your teaching, or the teaching at your school. You have tested it out with many students yourself and with other teachers teaching it also. You have also designed all the necessary resources and instructions.

If so, I congratulate you and wish you well as it is an exciting journey for you ahead!

However, you may be excited at the idea of franchising your music school but have yet to put together a unique program or method and are wondering how to get started.

Develop your own unique curriculum or method.

Here are my suggestions for getting started:

1. Take a look at all your local and relevant competitors and see if you can find something they have missed.
2. Take a look at all your local and relevant competitors and see if you can find something they are doing that inspires you.
3. Review your own skills and develop something around your strongest skills.
4. Review your favourite musical activities and develop something around them.
5. Include discussions with your students, friends, family, network and explore ideas.

Alternately you may decide not to franchise and instead, keep it simple and open multiple studios that you maintain ownership of but employ managers to take care of the day to day tasks.

POSITIVES/BENEFITS OF VIRTUOSO LEVEL:

- Freedom to work on "big picture" plans
- Large staff creating greater flexibility in all areas
- Managers in place for daily administration
- Variety and choice of work tasks
- Consultants and freelance assistance
- Increased income
- Greater customer reach and impact
- Be seen as a leader

NEGATIVES /DISADVANTAGES OF VIRTUOSO LEVEL:

- Greater financial commitment
- Greater financial risk
- Increased responsibilities in all areas
- The continual demands of leadership
- Finding the correct people/franchisees and consultants

CASE STUDY

Music school franchises are not exactly common. There are some that may seem like a franchise but are actually a "licence" agreement which is similar but not as legally binding. In Australia, licence agreements are to be treated with great caution as they can be easily treated like a franchise and therefore breach franchise regulations and get you into all sorts of legal trouble!

An example of a successful "Virtuoso" who owns a music school franchise would be Paul Myatt of Forte School of Music.

Paul describes himself as a teacher, coach, writer, speaker and performer.

Paul is the founding director along with Gillian Erskine of Forte School of Music in Brisbane in 1994 and currently has over 4000 students in Australia, New Zealand and the United Kingdom.

Paul is also the co-writer of the easiLEARNmusic range of music education books and a regular workshop presenter and speaker. He also continues to perform in a cabaret act called 2 Pauls and sings in the Sydney Philharmonia Choirs Symphony Chorus.

Paul says

> *"When we started Forte, we wanted to offer high quality, pedagogically sound courses and content where children loved learning within a business system that was able to be replicated."*

Other music school franchises to take a look at for ideas whether franchising might suit you, include:

- The Music Bus (Australia),
- Mini Maestros (Australia),
- Bach to Rock (US),
- Spaulding School of Music (Canada),
- Rock House (US)
- School of Rock (US)
- My Music Workshop (US)

VIRTUOSO LEVEL PROBLEM – Keeping your business "fresh"

It takes a huge effort in skill, time, energy and money to develop a large organisation such as a franchise or a multi-location music school. The problem however is that having put it all together -, the business systems, the teaching programs, the marketing, HR, etc etc - does not mean that the work is done and you can sit back and let others do the work.

All businesses, but particularly large businesses, need to ensure they are keeping systems and procedures up to date. In addition the products and services you offer need to be kept up to date to remain competitive with the "One Person Show" or "Leading Person" studios who can add and change programs almost on the spot!

SOLUTION

Keep your technology up to date and make sure your staff have access to the latest training. Maintain reviews of your competitors and allow time for creative brainstorming to keep programs and services constantly developing.

VIRTUOSO TO ICON ACTION STEPS:

"I am able to control multiple teams."

1. HR – Maintain, review and grow
2. IT – Maintain, review and grow
3. Ops – Maintain, review and grow
4. Fin – Maintain, review and grow
5. Leg – Maintain, review and grow
6. Merch – Maintain, review and grow
7. A and M – Maintain, review and grow
8. IP – Maintain, review and grow

CHAPTER 18

THE ICON

What makes an ICON?
To describe a person as an Icon, means they are important as a symbol of a particular thing, a representative of high standing within their industry.

In the case of the Music School Success ladder, we are referring to someone at Icon Level as a person who represents music education in many ways and is also so highly respected and well known, as to be in demand to offer opinion perhaps at government or certainly association level. An Icon may also be an advocate for music education in the media, internationally and so forth to such a degree that the mention of their name is immediately associated with music education.

It is hard to describe a "typical" person at ICON Level as it is rarely achieved.

It may be that they are a franchisor or owner of multiple studios as described at Virtuoso Level, but they would additionally need to be a prominent performer, author or such. The most obvious difference between an ICON and a VIRTUOSO though would be that an Icon is one those people with "celebrity" status within their industry at the very least.

POSITIVES/BENEFITS OF ICON LEVEL:

- Has multiple income streams
- Has a personal manager
- Has a personal assistant
- Is sought after for events
- Seen as an "Influencer"

NEGATIVES /DISADVANTAGES OF ICON LEVEL:

- Privacy issues due to being a celebrity
- Juggling a variety of demands
- Balancing lifestyle
- Finding the "right" people to surround yourself with

CASE STUDY

Awarded an OAM (Queen's Birthday Honours) Richard Gill has loved teaching ever since he was given a taste to "mind" a class at age 14. His dedication was such that he studied at Alexander Mackie Teachers College, then Sydney Conservatorium, and later the Orff Institute in Salzburg.

Richard however has many "strings to his bow" which is typical of someone at ICON level.

Developing new ensembles and organisations has long been a part of his activity, starting with the Strathfield Symphony Orchestra in 1969. The SSO Sinfonia and a National Mentoring Program are also some of his many achievements.

Richard Gill has also shown himself to be a great leader. In 1985 Gill was appointed Dean of the Western Australian Conservatorium of

Music, Director of Chorus at the Australian Opera and Music Director of the Victorian Opera.

Conducting of course is yet another activity that Gill has excelled at. First with the Sydney Youth Orchestra, but including many major orchestras, operas and music theatre productions around Australia.

Richard Gill is well known as being an outspoken advocate for quality music education as evidenced by numerous TED talks available on YouTube. His reputation is extensive as seen by this quote:

> *"Perhaps it's just as well that Leonard Bernstein is dead, otherwise he'd probably have to relinquish his great reputation as a musical educator – or at least share it with Sydney's Richard Gill."* – John Carmody, *The Sun Herald*

ICON LEVEL PROBLEM – Being a Celebrity

Most of us would be aware of the difficulties that well-known celebrities within our western society experience.

Lack of privacy, paparazzi, stalkers are common for movie stars and rock stars, but does this also apply to music education Icons? Not to the same degree of course, however any well-known personality has the problem of not being able to be totally free to act naturally, go where they want, with whom and when they want, as they may be recognised and judged or photographed with the ultimate problem being the misuse/misleading of the public.

Having random people interrupting you asking for a signature or a photo must be nice the first few times, but could become annoying quite quickly!

There must be a certain pressure being a celebrity. A loss of freedom, despite the obvious benefits.

SOLUTION

Finding a trustworthy team around you to monitor social media (and other media), finding private hangouts to de-stress and having clear boundaries with friends and acquaintances.

MAINTAINING ICON LEVEL ACTION STEPS:

"I am a respected and in-demand expert."

1. Active networking and vigilant review systems
2. Strong leadership
3. Entrepreneurial attitude
4. Flexibility

PART 4

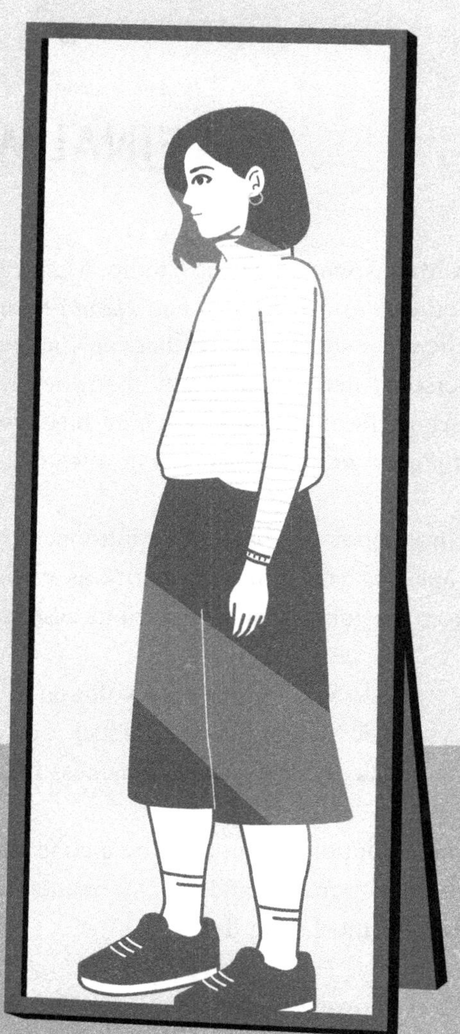

LAST BUT BY NO MEANS LEAST...

CHAPTER 19

A FINAL WORD

A Music School, Music Studio, Music Teaching Business (or whatever you like to call it), can and *should* be a constantly developing project. There are so many parts that can change over time, including your own personal needs and wants, that you should be prepared to adapt and change facets of your teaching business to make it suit you and your students and families in the best way possible.

Throughout this book, I've introduced you to my three systems in the hope that you will gain clarity as well as information and inspiration from my journey and the various case studies:

1. Music School Success Evolution
2. Music School Success Ladder
3. Music School Success Business Divisions

The evolution process can be a constant one, and should be a constant one as you review and adapt to make the best use of your resources and reap the most rewards.

I don't however want anyone reading this book to feel pressured by the MSS Ladder. I don't want anyone thinking they should be constantly expanding and trying to grow their studio, employ teachers or more teachers, open new locations and so on, if realistically all they want

(for example) is a reliable, efficient and enjoyable one person teaching studio based at home. The level you choose to move to on the MSS ladder should be one that you feel comfortable with and that provides you with all that you desire.

No matter what level on the MSS Ladder you wish to achieve though, it is important to keep reviewing the Eight Business Divisions for efficiency and suitability as time passes. A one person teaching studio ten years ago might have survived with no computer or internet use in lessons or for administration. These days it would not be an efficient way of running operations, and would possibly limit the enjoyment and interaction of students and impact on the marketing reach for that teacher.

Planning and reviewing are two of the most important tasks of any business owner and essential for those who want a profitable business!

Success looks different to everyone.

- Success can be found in sharing the joy music gives.
- Success can be in your students achievements – exams, scholarships, competitions and skills.
- Success can be felt when a student's social skills or confidence increases and their life improves.
- Success can also be seen as how many students you have, how much money you earn and how much profit there is at the end of it all.

Despite the title of this book *Music Teaching Made Profitable*, I encourage you to consider what music teaching success looks like to you when you are not considering money and profit. Without the feeling of success from a job well done, a student's life impacted, or opportunities of sharing some musical joy, you may not feel fulfilled.

I urge you to use this book thoroughly, come back to it repeatedly and most importantly take action one small step at a time. It is only through taking action, such as taking time to dream, or plan or build, that you can change your current situation. If you need help, or would like to share your success stories, I would love to hear from you. Look me up on Facebook or visit my website www.WendysMusic.com.au

Yours musically

Wendy

ABOUT THE AUTHOR

WENDY BRENTNALL-WOOD

Music Lover, Music Teacher, Music Author and Music Businesswoman

Wendy is the founder and director of Music School Success, a business that coaches music teachers to turn their passion into their own profitable venture.

Music is (and always has been) Wendy's passion even before she first started learning the piano as a child. That learning expanded over the years to include the clarinet, percussion instruments, guitar, oboe, violin and pipe organ.

A Melbourne University Conservatorium of Music graduate, Wendy has spent her lifetime overcoming many challenges to make her passion for music her career.

Her musical journey over the past three decades has included teaching private music classes, running and managing her own music teaching businesses, as well as holding music teaching positions at various Victorian primary and secondary schools. She has also directed choirs, string orchestras, concert bands, founded and directed a piano eisteddfod, coordinated church music and performed in various ensembles.

In among all that, she has written and self-published over 110 music teaching method books and launched an online video music performance competition.

Challenges she has overcome along the way include surviving Black Saturday (but almost losing her house in the process), as well as the inevitable struggles of juggling business and family life.

Wendy has served as a board member for Community Music Victoria and ANZCA as well as several arts and business committees and is a regular workshop presenter at various national music conferences.

Besides her various music interests and ventures, Wendy's other passions include her family (husband Howard, daughters Jessica and Cara, and son James), her dog (a Collie/Kelpie cross named Murphy) and cats (Archie, Ruby and daughter's cat Jet). She also has a soft spot for BMWs.

RECOMMENDED SUCCESS RESOURCES

RECOMMENDED SUCCESS RESOURCES

I've heard great teachers being called "Leading Learners", which seems very apt. Great teachers are always reading, networking, researching, exploring and discovering more so they can provide the best learning opportunities for their students but also for their own interests.

It has been mentioned in several places throughout this book, of the value of research and networks, so this Resource section is just a starting point if you need it, of places and people who can help.

Music Teacher Associations, Instrumental and Ensemble associations will provide things like:

- Workshops
- Conferences
- Newsletters
- Blogs
- Directory advertising
- Support systems

In most cases there is a relatively small annual fee to be a member and in some cases that will also entitle you to discounts from relevant suppliers.

This is by no means a complete list, but hopefully there will be one or more associations, societies or connections listed here that will be worthy of a look and getting in touch with for help to find the group for you.

Consider what it would be like if you had someone who cared enough about the outcome to look at your personal situation and help you make improvements to improve your circumstance. It's the fastest way to success, so I've also included in this resource section a link to my personalised coaching sessions.

Lastly there is a suggested reading and listening list. I've kept it short so you don't get overwhelmed by the amazing number of interesting books and podcasts out there. Use these to start building ideas for what is possible, or for specific details on a task, but most of all keep researching and planning what you want your life to look like with a Profitable Music School or Music Teaching Business.

Good luck and enjoy!

Imagine what you could accomplish working with your own personal music teaching/school Coach...

I have been working with, employing, training, mentoring and coaching musicians and music teachers for decades, and one thing has become very clear to me. After working with people at all different stages of their teaching journey, I've found that the lack of "taking action" is one of the most common issues.

Sometimes this lack of "action" to make change is due to lack of knowledge. They aren't aware of the choices.

Sometimes this lack of "action" to make change is due to lack of confidence. They don't have a strong support network which understands.

The fact is that to be a musician, you have already shown enormous application to learning your skill. Years of constant training and ongoing learning are required to develop an even intermediate skill level, and many of those reading this book are likely to be advanced musicians and professional performers!

You've proven to yourself and the world you are dedicated and intelligent yet for some reason your music school, or teaching business is just not achieving what you want. It might be that you are lacking the support of someone who knows and understands what running a music school is about. There are plenty of business coaches and courses available, but few with the detailed knowledge and understanding of our industry.

Having a coach and mentor can keep you accountable – help you to take the action needed to achieve your goals, but with someone there to lean on, someone who knows the pitfalls and can save you the time and trouble of making those mistakes.

So if you're really serious about taking your business and life to a higher level...

talk to Wendy about her personalised Coaching Sessions.

Private, confidential and effective.

www.WendysMusic.com.au/music-school-success/

ASSOCIATION LISTINGS

NATIONAL MUSIC TEACHERS ASSOCIATIONS

Australian Music Association (AMA
www.australianmusic.asn.au/ 03 9254 1019 info@australianmusic.asn.au

International Society for Music Education (ISME)
www.isme.org/

Australian Society for Music Education (ASME)
www.asme.edu.au/

Music Teachers National Association – U.S. (MTNA)
www.mtna.org/

National Association for Music Education – U.S. (NAFME)
www.nafme.org/

New Zealand Music Teachers (MENZA)
www.menza.co.nz/

Singapore Music Teachers' Association (SMTA)
www.smtasingapore.com/

Philippine Society for Music Education (PSME)
www.psme-online.org

Malaysian Association for Music Education (MAME)
www.mamebaru.org/

Indonesian Music Teachers Society
www.pypduniamusic.weebly.com/

Japanese Piano Teachers Association (JPTA)
www.jpta.jp/

Southeast Asia Directors of Music (SEADOM)
www.seadom.org/

Music Teachers Association – U.K.
www.musicteachers.org/

Society for Music Education in Ireland (SMEI)
www.smei.ie/

Scottish Association for Music Education (SAME)
www.same.org.uk/

European Music Educators Association (EMEA)
www.emeamusic.org/

European Chamber Music Teachers Association (ECMTA)
www.ecmta.eu/

European Piano Teachers (EPTA)
www.epta-europe.org/

European String Teachers (ESTA)
www.estastrings.org/

Music Teachers Association of India (MTAIND)
www.facebook.com/MTAIND/

AUSTRALIAN STATE MUSIC TEACHER ASSOCIATIONS

Victorian Music Teachers' Association (VMTA)
www.vmta.org.au/
03 5243 4200 Email: vmta@vmta.org.au

Music Teachers' Association of New South Wales (music NSW)
www.musicnsw.com.au/

Western Australian Music Teachers' Association (WAMTA)
www.musicteacherswa.org.au/

The Music Teachers' Association of South Australia (MTASA)
www.mtasa.com.au/

Queensland Music Teachers' Association (QMTA)
www.mtaq.org.au/

Tasmanian Music Teachers' Association (TMTA)
www.tmta.com.au

AUSTRALIAN NATIONAL INSTRUMENTAL GROUPS

The Australian Strings Association (AUSTA)
www.austa.asn.au
03 94430234 Email: admin@austa.asn.au
PO Box 187, Brunswick East, VIC 3057

Australian National Association of Teachers of Singing (ANATS)
www.anats.org.au/

Australian Flute Society (AFS)
www.australianflutesociety.org.au/

Australian Band and Orchestra Directors Association (ABODA)
www.aboda.org.au

Australian Guitar Societies
www.australianguitarist.com/guitar-societies/

SUGGESTED READING & LISTENING LIST

Business Books

The E-Myth series of books — Michael Gerber

Franchise Relationships and other books — Greg Nathan

The Success Principles and other books — Jack Canfield

The Millionaire Masterplan — Roger James Hamilton

The Seven Spiritual Laws of Success and other books — Deepak Chopra

Rich Dad, Poor Dad — Robert Kiyosaki

The Magician's Way — William Whitecloud

Money, Master the Game — Tony Robbins

Botty's Rules — Nigel Botterill

Think and Grow Rich — Napoleon Hill

Make Your Idea Matter and other books — Bernadette Jiwa

Business Podcasts

Online Marketing Made Easy

The Mind Your Business Podcast

Smart Passive Income

The Mentor Mark Bouris

Uncensored Growth

Mind Her Business

Music Teaching Books

The Practice Revolution — Philip Johnson

The Dynamic Studio — Philip Johnson

Perfect Pitch in the Key of Autism — Henny Kupferstein and Susan Cancer

The Virtuoso Teacher and other books — Paul Harris

The Savvy Music Teacher — David Cutler

Music Teaching Podcasts

Music Tech Teacher — Tim Topham AMusEd

Creative Piano Teaching Podcast

Talking Up Music Education

The Musicality Podcast

Parent Piano Podcast

www.ingramcontent.com/pod-product-compliance
Lightning Source LLC
Chambersburg PA
CBHW061045110426
42740CB00049B/2197

9781925288841